The Pampered Chef®

stoneware
inspirations

For twenty-five years, home cooks have turned to The Pampered Chef® for products and recipes that inspire at-home meal preparation. Our Family Heritage® Stoneware Collection forms the foundation of this rich tradition. And now, The Pampered Chef® Test Kitchens are proud to introduce an inspiring collection of recipes that highlight our Classics® and New Traditions™ Stoneware. Inside, you'll find over 60 delicious Stoneware recipes that make mealtimes easier for you and more enjoyable for your family. In addition, we've included tips and an expanded use and care section to make the most of your Stoneware.

This cookbook is part of a milestone year for The Pampered Chef®. We are confident that the recipes in this cookbook will help you to celebrate your own milestones with your family in the years ahead.

Enjoy!

The Pampered Chef® Test Kitchens

On the cover: *Shrimp-Stuffed Portobello Mushrooms* (p. 97)

The Pampered Chef is the premier direct-seller of high-quality kitchen tools sold through in-home Kitchen Shows. We are committed to enhancing family life by providing quality kitchen products supported by service and information for our Kitchen Consultants and customers.

contents

something sweet...70

Passing up dessert is out of the question when you serve one of these tempting cakes, cookies or other special treats from your kitchen with love. Stoneware makes baking so easy, the hardest part will be deciding which dessert to make first!

NEW CHAPTER! | table for two...94

The recipes in this chapter will put an end to repeat leftovers. Serve restaurant-quality appetizers, main dishes, brunches and desserts at home with these recipes specially tailored for two servings.

sensational, inspirational
stoneware

Getting to Know Your Stoneware

Family Heritage® Stoneware is made from natural stoneware clay. It is fired at temperatures of over 2000 degrees Fahrenheit to create a buff-colored Stoneware that is safe to use with food. Each piece of Family Heritage® Stoneware is hand finished, producing a one-of-a-kind creation. Our Classics® Collection is unglazed; the New Traditions™ Collection is glazed on the exterior only. Both offer the same baking performance by absorbing and retaining heat to produce more evenly baked foods. Just like a professional brick-lined oven, our Stoneware produces crisp crusts with less risk of burning, baked goods with moist interiors, and juicy, flavorful meats.

Preparing and Seasoning Your Stoneware for Use

Before using your Stoneware for the first time, we recommend that you rinse it in warm water, then towel dry.

When you season Stoneware for the first time, it begins the natural seasoning process—becoming stick-resistant as fats and oils from foods gradually adhere to the surface of the Stoneware. To season Stoneware, bake a high-fat food, such as refrigerated dinner rolls or cookie dough, on its surface. It is not necessary to re-season Stoneware before every use; however, if food does stick slightly, lightly apply vegetable oil to the surface for the next few uses. As Stoneware becomes increasingly seasoned, its color will gradually change from buff to a natural, deep brown. In fact, the performance of Stoneware will improve as the surface becomes darker.

Congratulations! You are a proud owner of one or more pieces in The Pampered Chef® Family Heritage® Stoneware Collection. It means you have an eye for quality, value and performance. Whether you are just beginning to collect Stoneware or you already have a number of our Classics® or New Traditions™ pieces, make the most of your investment by using this cookbook. Let it inspire the creative cook in you! But before turning your culinary inspirations loose in the kitchen, take a few moments to familiarize yourself with Stoneware, its unique qualities and how to care for the Family Heritage® Collection. Even if you're an experienced Stoneware user, these hints will enhance your culinary success.

Guidelines for Using Your Stoneware

It is very important to remember that Stoneware doesn't like extreme and sudden temperature changes, or what is called thermal shock. Despite its durability, Stoneware may develop small hairline cracks or even break if exposed to sudden temperature changes. By practicing the following guidelines, you will enjoy your Stoneware for years.

- Always preheat the oven before baking foods in Stoneware. However, do *not* preheat empty Stoneware in the oven because this may cause the Stoneware to crack or break.

- Stoneware cannot be used under the broiler or directly over a heat source such as a stovetop burner.

- Thick, dense frozen foods, such as chicken pieces, fish fillets or pork chops should be thawed completely before baking. Putting a frozen pizza or frozen precooked foods such as chicken nuggets, French fries and fish sticks on Stoneware is fine. Place the frozen food on the baking stone while preheating the oven and be sure to distribute small pieces evenly over the surface of the Stoneware.

- Use the same baking times and temperatures with Stoneware as you would with other bakeware. If you are preparing foods that require a short baking time (10 minutes or less, such as some cookies), you may need to bake them for 1 to 2 minutes longer. This may also apply to baked goods in higher altitudes.

- When using Stoneware in a convection oven, remember to reduce the oven temperature and baking time by the amount specified in the use and care manual for your oven.

- Stoneware is microwave-safe; however, a microwave cannot provide the same browning, texture, or even cooking as conventional or convection ovens.

- Stoneware should fit comfortably in your oven and not touch the sides or oven door when closed.

- Stoneware becomes extremely hot both in the oven and microwave oven. Always use heavy, heat-resistant oven mitts or oven pads when handling hot Stoneware.

- Due to its unique properties, Stoneware will remain hot for a longer period of time than other bakeware. Protect surfaces from heat or scratching by placing a protective barrier between the piece of Stoneware and the surface.

- Foods may be cut and served directly from Stoneware. Knives or other metal edges will not harm the Stoneware surface.

It's Time to Start Baking

Now that you're an expert on Stoneware, it's time to start baking. Leave it to The Pampered Chef® to guide you through effortless preparation while inspiring you. We know you will be delighted by the superb baking results of your Family Heritage® Stoneware. Enjoy!

Stoneware Volume Chart

The chart below highlights the volume of our Stoneware pieces. You will find that many recipes in this book contain helpful tips that allow you to scale recipes up or down to fit into other Stoneware pieces. See "Stoneware Substitution Tips" (below) for additional guidelines.

STONEWARE PIECE	VOLUME	STONEWARE PIECE	VOLUME
Small Bar Pan (6¼ x 8¾ inches)	1 cup	Stoneware Bar Pan (10 x 15½ inches)	6 cups
Small Oval Baker (4½ x 7¼ inches)	2 cups	Stoneware Loaf Pan (5 x 9 inches)	6 cups
Medium Bar Pan (7¾ x 11½ inches)	4 cups	Oval Baker (8 x 12 inches)	7 cups
Mini-Baker (8-inch round)	4 cups	Mini Fluted Pan (six 4-inch wells)	7½ cups
Stoneware Muffin Pan (twelve 2¾-inch wells)	4 cups	New Traditions™ Deep Dish Baker (11-inch round)	8 cups
Classic Deep Dish Baker (11-inch round)	6 cups	Square Baker (9 x 9 inches)	11 cups
Deep Dish Pie Plate (9-inch round)	6 cups	Stoneware Fluted Pan (9½-inch round)	11 cups
Mini Loaf Pan (four 2¼ x 5-inch wells)	6 cups	Rectangular Baker (9 x 13 inches)	14 cups

Stoneware Substitution Tips

• The key to successful substitution is to make sure the food will fill the substituted pan to the same volume as the original recipe. Make sure that foods do not fill the baker too full or they might bubble over during baking.

• When substituting Stoneware pieces, watch foods carefully and check for doneness and/or proper internal temperature.

• When food is spread more thinly over a larger surface, the oven temperature may need to be increased, and the bake time may need to be decreased to prevent the food from drying out. On the contrary, when food is spread more thickly over a smaller surface, the oven temperature may need to be decreased, and the bake time may need to be increased to allow the center of the food to bake through.

• Certain types of recipes, such as cakes and quick breads, perform better in some shapes of bakers or pans than others. When baking these types of recipes, make sure to fill the baker or pan 2/3 full with batter.

• For recipes that do not rise significantly, such as casseroles and dips, fill the baker about 3/4 full or no less than 1 inch from the top.

Cleaning and Handling Your Stoneware

Cleaning Stoneware is easy. To keep the seasoned surface intact, only gentle cleaning is required. Use of soap and detergent to clean Stoneware is not recommended. Soap will attach to the fats and oils in the seasoning and may remain on the surface, giving a soapy flavor to the next foods baked on it. Stoneware should not be washed in the dishwasher. We recommend a few simple steps for cleaning and handling:

• Always allow Stoneware to cool to room temperature before washing.

• Rinse under hot water and scrape off any excess food using the **Nylon Pan Scraper** (included with most Stoneware) or kitchen brush.

• If necessary, soak in clear, hot water to loosen baked-on foods, then rinse and dry thoroughly.

• To prevent Stoneware from cracking or breaking, be careful not to drop Stoneware or knock it against a hard surface.

• Avoid stacking or placing other heavy utensils, such as bowls or cookware, on top of Stoneware.

• If you store Stoneware on a rack in the oven, be sure to remove the pieces before turning on the oven.

easy appetizers

From momentous occasions to impromptu gatherings, this versatile collection of appetizers will fit into any menu.

Apricot-Almond Baked Brie (p. 10),
Tangy Bacon Roll-Ups (p. 11)

Apricot-Almond Baked Brie

*Elegant enough to serve at a cocktail party, this warm appetizer
is perfect for busy hosts who want to impress.*

PREP TIME: 15 MINUTES   BAKE TIME: 30-35 MINUTES   STAND TIME: 15 MINUTES

Brie and Camembert are French cheeses known for their soft texture and downy, white rind. When preparing these cheeses, leave the rind on the cheese. The entire cheese is edible, including the rind.

If desired, 1 package (8 ounces) cream cheese can be substituted for the Brie or Camembert cheese.

To store fresh parsley, wash it under cold running water, shake off excess moisture and wrap in paper towels. Store it in a resealable plastic food storage bag in the refrigerator up to 1 week.

Dijon mustard originally comes from Dijon, France. It is made from brown mustard seeds, white wine, unfermented grape juice and a blend of seasonings.

¼ **cup finely diced dried apricots**
¼ **cup almonds, chopped**
1 **tablespoon snipped fresh parsley**
2 **tablespoons apricot preserves**
1 **teaspoon Dijon mustard**
1 **package (8 ounces) refrigerated crescent rolls**
1 **4-inch round (8 ounces) Brie or Camembert cheese, rind included**
1 **egg, lightly beaten**
   Apple or pear wedges (optional)

1. Preheat oven to 350°F. Finely dice apricots using **Chef's Knife**. Chop almonds using **Food Chopper**. Snip parsley using **Kitchen Shears**. In **Small Batter Bowl**, combine apricots, almonds, parsley, preserves and mustard; mix well.

2. Unroll crescent dough on lightly floured **Cutting Board**. Separate dough crosswise into two squares, pressing seams to seal. Place Brie on one square of dough; set aside remaining square of dough. Trim corners from first dough square, leaving about a 1-inch border around Brie. Using **Medium Scoop**, scoop apricot mixture evenly over top of Brie.

3. Using **Creative Cutters**, cut one shape from each corner and center of remaining square of dough; set shapes aside. Trim corners of dough. Place dough over Brie, pinching seams to seal, if necessary. Fold and crimp edges of dough to seal. Using **Large Serving Spatula**, transfer Brie to **Small Round Stone**. Brush egg over entire surface of dough using **Pastry Brush**. Place cut-out shapes over dough; brush with egg. Bake 30-35 minutes or until crust is deep golden brown. Remove from oven to **Stackable Cooling Rack**; let stand 15 minutes before serving. Serve with apple or pear wedges, if desired.

Yield: 12 servings

Nutrients per serving: Calories 180, Total Fat 11 g, Saturated Fat 3.5 g, Cholesterol 30 mg, Carbohydrate 13 g, Protein 6 g, Sodium 280 mg, Fiber less than 1 g

Diabetic exchanges per serving: 1 starch, ½ high-fat meat, 1 fat (1 carb)

Variations: *Jalapeño Baked Brie:* Omit mustard. Substitute finely diced green bell pepper for the apricots, chopped pecans for the almonds and jalapeño jelly for the apricot preserves. Proceed as recipe directs.

Cranberry-Walnut Baked Brie: Omit mustard. Substitute sweetened dried cranberries for the apricots, chopped walnuts for the almonds and currant jelly for the apricot preserves. Proceed as recipe directs.

Tangy Bacon Roll-Ups

These sweet and smoky bites will be a hit at your next party.

PREP TIME: 15 MINUTES BAKE TIME: 18-20 MINUTES

2 **cans (8 ounces each) whole water chestnuts (30 water chestnuts), drained**

1 **package (2.1 ounces) fully cooked bacon slices (15 slices)**

½ **cup packed brown sugar**

½ **cup ketchup**

1 **tablespoon cider vinegar**

1 **teaspoon Dijon mustard**

2 **garlic cloves, pressed**

1. Preheat oven to 400°F. Line **Medium Bar Pan** with an 11-inch piece of **Parchment Paper**; set aside. Drain water chestnuts using small **Colander**; set aside. Cut bacon slices crosswise in half using **Kitchen Shears**. Wrap bacon slice around each water chestnut; secure with a wooden pick.

2. In **Small (2-qt.) Saucepan**, combine brown sugar, ketchup, vinegar, mustard and garlic pressed with **Garlic Press**. Bring to a boil over medium heat; reduce heat to medium-low and cook 5 minutes, or until sauce thickens, stirring occasionally. Remove from heat.

3. Carefully dip each wrapped water chestnut into sauce; gently tap against edge of saucepan to remove excess sauce and place on pan. Bake 18-20 minutes or until sauce is thick and darkened. Remove pan from oven to **Stackable Cooling Rack**. Carefully remove water chestnuts to serving platter. Serve warm.

Yield: 30 appetizers

| LIGHT | Nutrients per serving (3 appetizers): Calories 100, Total Fat 2.5 g, Saturated Fat 1 g, Cholesterol 10 mg, Carbohydrate 17 g, Protein 3 g, Sodium 260 mg, Fiber 2 g |

Diabetic exchanges per serving (3 appetizers): 1 starch, ½ fat (1 carb)

Fully cooked bacon slices are a convenient food product for people on the go. They can be found in the deli section by the other packaged meats at most grocery stores. If you cannot find fully cooked bacon slices, cook and drain 15 slices of uncooked bacon and proceed as recipe directs.

Lining your Stoneware with Parchment Paper makes cleanup a breeze.

Fantastic Focaccia Bread

Italian flair and flavors abound in this garlicky, cheesy flat bread.

PREP TIME: 10 MINUTES   BAKE TIME: 25-28 MINUTES

1 package (13.8 ounces) refrigerated
   pizza crust
2 garlic cloves, pressed
²/₃ cup (2 ounces) grated fresh Romano
   or Parmesan cheese, divided
2 cups (8 ounces) shredded
   mozzarella cheese, divided
2 teaspoons dried oregano leaves,
   divided
2 firm plum tomatoes, sliced

1. Preheat oven to 375°F. Roll out pizza crust to
   within 1 inch of edge of **Rectangle Stone**
   using lightly floured **Baker's Roller**™. Press
   garlic over crust using **Garlic Press**; spread
   evenly using **Skinny Scraper**.

2. Grate half of the Romano cheese over crust
   using **Deluxe Cheese Grater**. Sprinkle with
   half of the mozzarella cheese and
   1 teaspoon of the oregano. Thinly slice
   tomatoes with **Ultimate Slice & Grate** fitted
   with adjustable thin slicing blade; arrange in a
   single layer over cheese. Top with the
   remaining mozzarella cheese and oregano.
   Grate the remaining Romano cheese
   over top.

3. Bake 25-28 minutes or until crust is golden
   brown and cheese is bubbly. Cut into squares
   with **Pizza Cutter**; serve hot using **Mini-
   Serving Spatula**.

Yield: 24 appetizers

Nutrients per serving (2 appetizers): Calories 160, Total Fat 6 g,
Saturated Fat 3 g, Cholesterol 15 mg, Carbohydrate 17 g,
Protein 10 g, Sodium 370 mg, Fiber less than 1 g

Diabetic exchanges per serving (2 appetizers): 1 starch,
1 medium-fat meat (1 carb)

cook's tips

This recipe can be made
on the **Classic Round
Stone**. Roll pizza crust
to a 12-inch circle;
proceed as recipe
directs.

There's no need to peel
garlic cloves when using
the **Garlic Press**. When
cloves are pressed, the
garlic flesh gets forced
through the holes, while
the papery skin stays in
the hopper.

Spicy Chicken Wings

Subtly spicy with a tangy sauce, these appetizer wings are reminiscent of chicken tikka, a popular Indian dish flavored with yogurt and spices.

PREP TIME: 10 MINUTES   MARINATE TIME: 3 HOURS OR OVERNIGHT   BAKE TIME: 45-50 MINUTES

Marinade and Wings

- 1 **cup low-fat plain yogurt**
- 4 **teaspoons ground cumin**
- 4 **teaspoons curry powder**
- 4 **garlic cloves, pressed**
- 1 **teaspoon salt**
- 1/4-1/2 **teaspoon cayenne pepper**
- 26 **chicken wingettes or drumettes (about 2 1/2 pounds)**

Sauce

- 2 **limes**
- 1 **tablespoon snipped fresh cilantro**
- 3/4 **cup apricot preserves**

1. For marinade, combine yogurt, cumin, curry powder, garlic pressed with **Garlic Press**, salt and cayenne pepper in **Stainless (2-qt.) Mixing Bowl**; mix well. Rinse chicken; pat dry with paper towels. Place chicken and marinade in resealable plastic food storage bag; turn to coat. Marinate in refrigerator 3 hours or overnight.

2. For sauce, zest limes using **Lemon Zester/Scorer** to measure 1 teaspoon zest. Juice limes using **Juicer** to measure 1/4 cup juice. Snip cilantro using **Kitchen Shears**. Combine zest, juice, cilantro and preserves in **Small Batter Bowl**; mix well. Cover; refrigerate until ready to serve.

3. When ready to bake, preheat oven to 375°F. Line **Stoneware Bar Pan** with a 17-inch piece of **Parchment Paper**. Remove chicken from marinade; discard plastic bag with marinade. Arrange chicken in single layer on Parchment Paper. Bake 45-50 minutes or until chicken is no longer pink and skin is golden brown; remove from oven. Remove chicken to serving platter; serve warm with sauce.

Yield: 12 servings

Nutrients per serving: Calories 170, Total Fat 7 g, Saturated Fat 2 g, Cholesterol 30 mg, Carbohydrate 15 g, Protein 10 g, Sodium 135 mg, Fiber 0 g

Diabetic exchanges per serving: 1 starch, 1 medium-fat meat (1 carb)

You can ask your butcher to cut chicken wings into wingettes or drumettes. Or you can easily do it yourself by cutting chicken wings at joints, discarding the tip section.

This recipe can be easily cut in half and baked on the **Medium Bar Pan**. For marinade, combine 1/2 cup plain yogurt, 2 teaspoons pressed garlic cloves, 2 teaspoons ground cumin, 2 teaspoons curry powder, 1/2 teaspoon salt and 1/8 teaspoon cayenne pepper. Marinate 12 chicken wingettes or drumettes as recipe directs. Bake at 375°F 30-35 minutes. For sauce, combine 1/3 cup apricot preserves, 2 tablespoons lime juice, 1/2 teaspoon lime zest and 1 1/2 teaspoons fresh snipped cilantro.

Artichoke & Sun-Dried Tomato Tart

The crowning touch of this savory appetizer is the flaky, crispy phyllo shell.

PREP TIME: 15 MINUTES   BAKE TIME: 28-30 MINUTES

1 package (8 ounces) cream cheese, softened

1 egg

2 tablespoons all-purpose flour

1 jar (6 ounces) marinated artichokes, drained and patted dry

1/3 cup oil-packed sun-dried tomatoes, drained and patted dry

2 tablespoons snipped fresh basil leaves

1 cup (4 ounces) shredded mozzarella cheese

1 garlic clove, pressed

1/4 cup (1 ounce) grated fresh Parmesan cheese, divided

8 sheets (9 x 14 inches) thawed, frozen phyllo dough (see Cook's Tip)

Nonstick cooking spray

1 large plum tomato, sliced

Additional snipped basil (optional)

1. Preheat oven to 375°F. In **Classic Batter Bowl**, whisk cream cheese, egg and flour until smooth using **Stainless Whisk**. Chop artichokes using **Food Chopper**. Snip sun-dried tomatoes and basil using **Kitchen Shears**. Add artichokes, sun-dried tomatoes, basil, mozzarella cheese and garlic pressed with **Garlic Press** to cream cheese mixture; mix well.

2. Grate Parmesan cheese using **Deluxe Cheese Grater**; set aside 2 tablespoons for later use. Unroll phyllo. Lay one sheet of phyllo on **Large Grooved Cutting Board** and spray with nonstick cooking spray. Sprinkle with one-fourth of the remaining Parmesan cheese. Place second sheet of phyllo over first, pressing sheets together to seal. Place phyllo sheets on **Small Round Stone** (edges will hang off stone). Repeat three more times, arranging phyllo sheets in an overlapping staggered pattern on baking stone.

3. Spoon cream cheese mixture onto center of phyllo and spread to within 1/2 inch of edge of baking stone using **Small Spreader**. Slice tomato using **Ultimate Slice & Grate** fitted with v-shaped blade; arrange in an overlapping circular pattern around edge of filling. Sprinkle with reserved 2 tablespoons of Parmesan cheese. Carefully lift edges of phyllo sheets up against edge of filling. Lightly spray phyllo with nonstick cooking spray. Bake 28-30 minutes or until phyllo is golden brown and filling is set in center. Remove from oven and let stand 10 minutes. Garnish with additional snipped basil, if desired. Cut into wedges using **Utility Knife**; serve warm or at room temperature.

Yield: 12 servings

Nutrients per serving: Calories 160, Total Fat 11 g, Saturated Fat 6 g, Cholesterol 45 mg, Carbohydrate 9 g, Protein 7 g, Sodium 240 mg, Fiber less than 1 g

Diabetic exchanges per serving: 1/2 starch, 1 medium-fat meat, 1 fat (1/2 carb)

Phyllo dough is an ingredient found in many Greek and Middle Eastern recipes. It is available in supermarkets in the frozen foods section. Before using, thaw phyllo dough according to package directions, about 12 hours in the refrigerator.

Keep phyllo sheets covered with plastic wrap while working on a recipe. Otherwise, phyllo may dry out and crack, becoming unusable.

Wrap any leftover phyllo tightly with plastic wrap and keep in your refrigerator for up to 2 weeks. For longer storage, wrap tightly in plastic wrap and freeze for up to 2 months.

Roasted Potato Bites

This unique appetizer takes the comfort of a baked potato with "the works" and spins it in a fresh, appealing way.

PREP TIME: 20 MINUTES   BAKE TIME: 30-32 MINUTES

12 "B" size red potatoes (about 2 inches in diameter), unpeeled

1 tablespoon olive or vegetable oil

2 garlic cloves, pressed

1/2 teaspoon salt

1/4 teaspoon ground black pepper

4 ounces chive and onion cream cheese spread

3 tablespoons sour cream

Optional toppings such as grated cheddar cheese, bacon bits and snipped fresh chives

1. Preheat oven to 425°F. Cut potatoes in half crosswise. Cut a thin slice off bottom of each potato half. Carefully scoop out a small amount of pulp from each potato half using **Cook's Corer**™. In **Classic Batter Bowl**, combine oil, garlic pressed with **Garlic Press**, salt and black pepper. Add potato halves; toss to coat.

2. Place potato halves, hollowed side down, on **Medium Bar Pan**. Bake 30-32 minutes or until deep golden brown and tender. Remove from oven; cool slightly.

3. In **Small Batter Bowl**, combine cream cheese spread and sour cream; whisk until smooth using **Stainless Whisk**. Attach desired tip to **Easy Accent® Decorator**; fill with cream cheese mixture and pipe evenly into hollowed potato halves. Sprinkle with toppings, if desired. Place on serving platter; serve slightly warm.

Yield: 24 appetizers

Nutrients per serving (2 appetizers): Calories 80, Total Fat 5 g, Saturated Fat 2.5 g, Cholesterol 10 mg, Carbohydrate 9 g, Protein 2 g, Sodium 150 mg, Fiber 1 g

Diabetic exchanges per serving (2 appetizers): 1/2 starch, 1 fat (1/2 carb)

cook's tips

"B" size potatoes are new red potatoes that measure about 2 inches in diameter. They are often found in bags by the other potatoes in most grocery stores.

The mid-sized Medium Bar Pan is perfect for preparing a variety of bite-sized appetizers, bar cookies, biscuits and brownie mixes (19-21 ounces). It is also ideal for frozen foods such as chicken patties and French bread pizzas.

Crab Rangoon Dip,
Crispy Wonton Chips (p. 22)

Create-a-Party Dip

Your guests will love any of the three delicious, warm dips offered here.

PREP TIME: 10 MINUTES   BAKE TIME: 22-25 MINUTES

Dip Base	1 package (8 ounces) cream cheese, softened		
	1 garlic clove, pressed		
	Goat Cheese Marinara Dip	**Fiesta Chicken Dip**	**Crab Rangoon Dip**
Cheese	4 ounces crumbled goat cheese	1 cup (4 ounces) shredded Mexican cheese blend	1 cup (4 ounces) shredded Swiss cheese
Sauce	1 cup marinara or pizza sauce	3/4 cup medium thick and chunky salsa	3/4 cup sweet and sour sauce
Toppings	1 jar (6 ounces) marinated artichoke hearts, drained, patted dry and chopped 1/4 cup chopped red bell pepper	1 cup chopped cooked chicken 1/4 cup sliced pitted ripe olives	1 cup chopped imitation crabmeat 1/4 cup sliced almonds
Garnish	2 tablespoons snipped fresh basil leaves	2 tablespoons snipped fresh cilantro	2 tablespoons thinly sliced green onions with tops
Chips (see p. 22)	*Rosemary Pita Chips*	*Lime Tortilla Chips*	*Crispy Wonton Chips*

1. Preheat oven to 350°F. In **Small Batter Bowl**, combine ***Dip Base*** ingredients. Add ***Cheese***; mix until well blended. Spread onto bottom of **Mini-Baker**.

2. Spoon ***Sauce*** over ***Cheese***. Sprinkle evenly with ***Toppings***.

3. Bake 22-25 minutes or until dip is heated through and outside edge is bubbly. Sprinkle with ***Garnish*** before serving, if desired. Serve warm with ***Chips***.

Yield: 14 servings (about 3 1/2 cups)

Nutrients per serving (1/4 cup dip):

Goat Cheese Marinara Dip	Fiesta Chicken Dip	Crab Rangoon Dip
Calories 90, Total Fat 8 g, Saturated Fat 4.5 g, Cholesterol 20 mg, Carbohydrate 3 g, Protein 3 g, Sodium 200 mg, Fiber less than 1 g	Calories 110, Total Fat 9 g, Saturated Fat 5 g, Cholesterol 35 mg, Carbohydrate 2 g, Protein 6 g, Sodium 210 mg, Fiber 0 g	Calories 120, Total Fat 9 g, Saturated Fat 5 g, Cholesterol 25 mg, Carbohydrate 6 g, Protein 5 g, Sodium 220 mg, Fiber 0 g
Diabetic exchanges per serving: 0 starch, 1 vegetable, 1 1/2 fat (0 carb)	Diabetic exchanges per serving: 0 starch, 1 medium-fat meat, 1 fat (0 carb)	Diabetic exchanges per serving: 0 starch, 1 vegetable, 1/2 low-fat meat, 1 1/2 fat (0 carb)

cook's tips

This recipe can be easily doubled and baked in the **Deep Dish Baker**, if desired. Bake at 350°F 25-30 minutes or until heated through.

Goat cheese is a white goat's milk cheese noted for its distinctive tart flavor. If desired, 4 ounces of cream cheese can be substituted for the goat cheese.

To save time before your party, purchase a rotisserie chicken the night before the event and remove the breast meat to yield 1 cup chopped chicken. The rest of the chicken can be served to your family the night before the party.

Chopped cooked shrimp or lump crabmeat can be substituted for the imitation crabmeat, if desired.

Easy Appetizers 21

30

minutes or less

Crushed dried rosemary can be substituted for the Rosemary Herb Seasoning Mix, if desired.

The **Citrus Press** makes juicing limes a quick and easy task. Simply slice a lime in half crosswise, place it into the hopper of the press and squeeze.

Wonton wrappers are paper-thin, 3½-inch square sheets of dough used to make filled wontons. They can be found in the produce section of most supermarkets.

Rosemary Pita Chips

   4 **whole wheat pita pocket bread rounds**

   4 **garlic cloves, pressed**

   1 **tablespoon olive oil**

   1 **tablespoon** *Pantry Rosemary Herb Seasoning Mix*

1. Preheat oven to 400°F. Split each pita pocket in half horizontally. Using **Garlic Press**, press garlic over pita rounds; spread evenly. Lightly spray rounds with oil using **Kitchen Spritzer**; sprinkle evenly with seasoning mix.

2. Cut each round into eight wedges. Arrange half of the pita wedges in a single layer on **Large Round Stone**. Bake 8-10 minutes or until chips are lightly browned and crisp. Remove from baking stone; cool completely. Repeat with remaining pita wedges.

Yield: 64 pita chips (16 servings)

| LIGHT | Nutrients per serving (4 chips): Calories 50, Total Fat 1.5 g, Saturated Fat 0 g, Cholesterol 0 mg, Carbohydrate 10 g, Protein 2 g, Sodium 150 mg, Fiber 1 g |

Diabetic exchanges per serving (4 chips): ½ starch (½ carb)

Lime Tortilla Chips

   8 **(7-inch) flour tortillas**

   2 **tablespoons lime juice**

   ¼ **teaspoon coarse salt**

1. Preheat oven to 400°F. Brush one side of each tortilla with lime juice; sprinkle lightly with salt. Cut each tortilla into eight wedges; arrange half of the tortilla wedges in a single layer on **Large Round Stone**. Bake 8-10 minutes or until edges are lightly browned and crisp.

2. Remove from baking stone; cool completely. Repeat with remaining tortilla wedges.

Yield: 64 chips (16 servings)

| LIGHT | Nutrients per serving (4 chips): Calories 40, Total Fat 1.5 g, Saturated Fat 0 g, Cholesterol 0 mg, Carbohydrate 6 g, Protein 1 g, Sodium 170 mg, Fiber less than 1 g |

Diabetic exchanges per serving (4 chips): ½ starch (½ carb)

Crispy Wonton Chips

   32 **square wonton wrappers**
       Nonstick cooking spray

1. Preheat oven to 375°F. Cut each wonton wrapper in half diagonally; arrange in a single layer on **Large Round Stone**. Spray with nonstick cooking spray.

2. Bake 8-10 minutes or until golden brown and crisp. Remove from baking stone; cool completely. Repeat with remaining wontons.

Yield: 64 chips (16 servings)

| LIGHT | Nutrients per serving (4 chips): Calories 40, Total Fat .5 g, Saturated Fat 0 g, Cholesterol 0 mg, Carbohydrate 7 g, Protein 1 g, Sodium 70 mg, Fiber 0 g |

Diabetic exchanges per serving (4 chips): ½ starch (½ carb)

Create-a-Crostini (pp. 24-25)

Create-a-Crostini

This easy appetizer is an ideal base for an assortment of toppings. Here are a few suggestions to create a trio of distinctively different, elegant crostini.

PREP AND BAKE TIME: 15-17 MINUTES

30

minutes or less

Crostini and cheese spread can be prepared ahead of time. Cool crostini completely and store in resealable plastic food storage bags for up to 1 day. Combine cheese spread ingredients; cover with lid and refrigerate until ready to use.

Pantry Basil Oil can be substituted for the olive oil when making *Tomato-Basil Crostini*, if desired.

These crostini would be a lovely addition to a tapas theme party. Tapas originated in Spain as appetizers served on small plates.

Crostini translates into "little toasts" in Italian and are small, thin slices of toasted bread that are brushed with olive oil.

Crostini

24   slices French bread, cut ¼ inch thick

2   tablespoons olive oil

Cheese Spread

1   package (8 ounces) cream cheese, softened

¼   cup mayonnaise

¼   teaspoon ground black pepper

1   garlic clove, pressed

Create-a-Flavor ingredients (see chart, opposite page)

1. Preheat oven to 375°F. For crostini, place bread slices on **Rectangle Stone**; lightly brush with oil. Bake 10-12 minutes or until light golden brown; cool completely.

2. For cheese spread, in **Classic Batter Bowl**, combine cream cheese, mayonnaise, black pepper and garlic pressed with **Garlic Press**. Add *Stir-In* (see chart at right).

3. To assemble, spread cheese spread over crostini; top with *Deli Meat*. In small bowl, combine *Topping* ingredients; spoon over deli meat. Sprinkle with *Garnish*.

Yield: 24 crostini

Create-a-Flavor

These flavorful ingredient combinations transform crostini into fanciful appetizers you'll want to share.

PREP TIME: 10 MINUTES

Flavor	Tomato-Basil Crostini	Roast Beef & Horseradish Crostini	Turkey & Cranberry Crostini
Stir-In	¼ cup finely snipped fresh basil	2 tablespoons prepared horseradish	¼ cup thinly sliced green onions with tops
Deli Meat	8 ounces thinly sliced deli chicken breast (optional)	8 ounces thinly sliced deli roast beef	8 ounces thinly sliced deli turkey breast
Toppings	4 plum tomatoes, seeded and diced 2 teaspoons balsamic vinegar Salt and ground black pepper to taste	½ cup finely diced roasted red bell pepper ½ cup finely diced red onion	½ cup finely diced dried apricots ½ cup apricot preserves ¼ cup sweetened dried cranberries
Garnish	¼ cup (2 ounces) grated fresh Parmesan cheese	1 tablespoon fresh snipped parsley	Toasted sliced almonds

Nutrients per serving (1 topped crostini):

Tomato-Basil Crostini	Roast Beef & Horseradish Crostini	Turkey & Cranberry Crostini
Calories 160, Total Fat 8 g, Saturated Fat 3 g, Cholesterol 10 mg, Carbohydrate 17 g, Protein 4 g, Sodium 290 mg, Fiber 1 g Diabetic exchanges per serving: 1 starch, ½ vegetable, 1½ fat (1 carb)	Calories 160, Total Fat 7 g, Saturated Fat 2.5 g, Cholesterol 15 mg, Carbohydrate 18 g, Protein 5 g, Sodium 310 mg, Fiber 1 g Diabetic exchanges per serving: 1 starch, ½ vegetable, 1½ fat (1 carb)	Calories 190, Total Fat 7 g, Saturated Fat 2.5 g, Cholesterol 15 mg, Carbohydrate 25 g, Protein 5 g, Sodium 330 mg, Fiber 1 g Diabetic exchanges per serving: 1 starch, ½ fruit, 1½ fat (1½ carb)

cook's tips

30 minutes or less

Gently wash fresh basil leaves just before using and blot dry with a paper towel. To store, wrap in a damp paper towel, place in a resealable plastic food storage bag and refrigerate up to 1 week.

To prevent sticking when dicing dried apricots, spray the **Chef's Knife** with a little nonstick cooking spray.

To toast almonds in the microwave oven, place almonds in **Small Oval Baker**; microwave on HIGH 5-7 minutes or until golden brown, stirring after each 30-second interval. Cool completely.

main dishes
& more

With more creative solutions than ever to the weekly meal-planning challenge, dinner has never been easier—or more delicious!

Balsamic & Onion Roast Chicken (p. 28),
Baked Parmesan Risotto (p. 29)

Balsamic & Onion Roast Chicken

This simple, savory roast chicken is the perfect size to serve half now and save the other half for two other delicious recipes later in the week.

PREP TIME: 15 MINUTES   BAKE TIME: 1 HOUR, 40 MINUTES TO 2 HOURS   STAND TIME: 10 MINUTES

Save half of the roasted chicken and vegetables for another day to make these recipes:

Chinese Chicken Pizza (p. 31)

Chicken & Broccoli Ring (p. 33)

1 large sweet onion, cut into
   1/2-inch slices

1/4 cup water

1 package (2.6 ounces) golden onion soup mix (2 envelopes)

1/4 cup white balsamic or white wine vinegar

1 tablespoon olive oil

2 teaspoons paprika

4 garlic cloves, pressed

1 roasting chicken (41/2-51/2 pounds)

1. Preheat oven to 400°F. Using **Chef's Knife**, cut onion into 1/2-inch-thick slices; arrange evenly over bottom of **Deep Dish Baker** and add water. In **Small Batter Bowl**, combine soup mix, vinegar, oil, paprika and garlic pressed with **Garlic Press**.

2. Remove and discard giblets and neck from chicken cavity. Rinse chicken with cold water; pat dry. Trim excess fat using **Kitchen Shears**, if necessary. Using **Pastry Brush**, brush soup mixture evenly over back side of chicken. Place chicken in baker, breast side up. Brush inside cavity of chicken with soup mixture. Tie ends of legs together with cotton string. Lift wing tips up toward neck then tuck under back of chicken. Brush remaining soup mixture evenly over outside of chicken.

3. Cover chicken loosely with aluminum foil. Bake 1 hour, 40 minutes to 2 hours or until **Pocket Thermometer** registers 180°F in meaty part of thigh and juices run clear. Remove foil during last 5-10 minutes of baking. Remove chicken from oven; transfer to **Reversible Bamboo Carving Board**. Tent with foil and let stand 10 minutes before carving.

4. Remove half of the onion slices (about 1/2 cup) from baker. Remove meat from half of chicken. Wrap and refrigerate chicken and onion slices up to 4 days to be used for *Chinese Chicken Pizza* and *Chicken & Broccoli Ring*.

5. Skim fat from juices and discard. Carve remaining half of chicken into thin slices. Serve chicken with remaining onions and pan juices.

Yield: 4 servings

Nutrients per serving: Calories 330, Total Fat 19 g, Saturated Fat 5 g, Cholesterol 100 mg, Carbohydrate 6 g, Protein 32 g, Sodium 250 mg, Fiber 0 g

Diabetic exchanges per serving: 1/2 starch, 4 medium-fat meat (1/2 carb)

Baked Parmesan Risotto

This easy rice dish will become a staple in your recipe repertoire. It can accompany just about any poultry dish you serve it with and can be dressed up or down to suit your needs.

PREP TIME: 10 MINUTES   BAKE TIME: 35-40 MINUTES

1/2   cup (2 ounces) grated fresh Parmesan cheese

1/4   cup chopped onion

2   cups milk

1   can (10 3/4 ounces) condensed cream of chicken soup

1   cup instant long-grain white rice

1/4   teaspoon salt

1/8   teaspoon ground black pepper

Additional grated fresh Parmesan cheese and snipped fresh parsley (optional)

1. Preheat oven to 375°F. Lightly spray **Mini-Baker** with nonstick cooking spray. Grate Parmesan cheese using **Deluxe Cheese Grater**. Chop onion using **Food Chopper**. In **Classic Batter Bowl**, combine milk, soup, rice, cheese, onion, salt and black pepper; mix well.

2. Pour rice mixture into baker. Bake 35-40 minutes or until bubbly around edges and all liquid is absorbed. Sprinkle with additional cheese and parsley, if desired.

Yield: 4 servings

Nutrients per serving: Calories 290, Total Fat 10 g, Saturated Fat 5 g, Cholesterol 25 mg, Carbohydrate 34 g, Protein 13 g, Sodium 1120 mg, Fiber 1 g

Diabetic exchanges per serving: 2 starch, 1 medium-fat meat, 1 fat (2 carb)

Risotto is traditionally a Northern Italian rice dish that is created by stirring hot stock into rice in batches as the rice cooks. This results in a creamy consistency. Here, we have created a shortcut to simplify the labor-intensive cooking technique.

This recipe can be doubled and baked in the **New Traditions™ Deep Dish Baker**.

Chinese Chicken Pizza

Leftovers become make-overs! It's amazing that an Asian-inspired dish can come out of leftover balsamic-glazed chicken.

PREP TIME: 10 MINUTES   BAKE TIME: 16-18 MINUTES

1/2 **cup onion slices from *Balsamic & Onion Roast Chicken* (p. 28), coarsely chopped**

1 1/2 **cups cooked chicken from *Balsamic & Onion Roast Chicken*, cubed**

1 **can (8 ounces) sliced water chestnuts, drained**

1/2 **cup teriyaki baste and glaze**

1 **medium red, yellow or green bell pepper, cut into 1-inch strips**

1 **package (10 ounces) prebaked thin pizza crust**

1 1/2 **cups (6 ounces) shredded mozzarella cheese, divided**

1. Preheat oven to 425°F. Using **Chef's Knife**, coarsely chop onion slices.

2. In **Classic Batter Bowl**, combine onion, chicken and water chestnuts. Add teriyaki baste and glaze and toss gently. Slice bell pepper into 1-inch strips; cut strips in half. Place pizza crust on **Large Round Stone**. Spoon chicken mixture evenly over crust to within 1/2 inch of edge. Sprinkle half of the cheese over chicken mixture; top evenly with bell pepper. Sprinkle with remaining cheese.

3. Bake 16-18 minutes or until cheese is melted and crust is deep golden brown. Remove from oven; let stand 5 minutes. Cut into wedges.

Yield: 6 servings

Nutrients per serving: Calories 360, Total Fat 12 g, Saturated Fat 5 g, Cholesterol 55 mg, Carbohydrate 40 g, Protein 23 g, Sodium 1070 mg, Fiber 2 g

Diabetic exchanges per serving: 2 1/2 starch, 2 medium-fat meat (2 1/2 carb)

minutes or less

Teriyaki baste and glaze is a thickened, bottled teriyaki sauce that can be found in the ethnic section of most grocery stores.

Water chestnuts are the tubers of a Southeast Asian water plant. They are unrelated to chestnuts, which are grown on trees. In the United States, water chestnuts are most commonly available in cans and are ready for cooking or eating raw.

Chicken & Broccoli Ring

This family-friendly dinner is made easy with the help of planned-over chicken from earlier in the week.

PREP TIME: 20 MINUTES   BAKE TIME: 25-30 MINUTES

1   package (8 ounces) refrigerated crescent rolls

1   cup coarsely chopped cooked chicken from *Balsamic & Onion Roast Chicken* (p. 28)

3/4   cup coarsely chopped broccoli

1/2   cup (2 ounces) shredded cheddar cheese

1/4   cup diced red bell pepper

2   tablespoons mayonnaise

1   teaspoon *Pantry All-Purpose Dill Mix*

1   small garlic clove, pressed

1/8   teaspoon salt

1   egg white, lightly beaten

2   tablespoons slivered almonds

1. Preheat oven to 375°F. Unroll crescent rolls; separate into eight triangles. Arrange triangles, slightly overlapping, in a circle on **Small Round Stone** with wide ends 3 inches from edge of baking stone (points will extend off the edge of the baking stone). Roll wide ends of dough toward center to create a 3-inch opening.

2. In **Classic Batter Bowl**, combine chicken, broccoli, cheese, bell pepper, mayonnaise, seasoning mix, garlic pressed with **Garlic Press** and salt; mix well.

3. Using **Large Scoop**, scoop filling evenly over dough in a continuous circle. Bring points of triangles up over filling and tuck under dough at center to form a ring. (Filling will show.) Lightly brush dough with egg white using **Pastry Brush**; sprinkle with almonds. Bake 25-30 minutes or until deep golden brown.

Yield: 4 servings

Nutrients per serving: Calories 430, Total Fat 27 g, Saturated Fat 8 g, Cholesterol 50 mg, Carbohydrate 25 g, Protein 20 g, Sodium 700 mg, Fiber less than 1 g

Diabetic exchanges per serving: 1½ starch, 1 vegetable, 2 medium-fat meat, 3 fat (1½ carb)

Dill weed is an herb with a fresh, distinctive flavor and has been used in cooking for thousands of years. Use it in salad dressings, breads, sauces and vegetables.

Dried dill weed can be substituted for the All-Purpose Dill Mix, if desired.

The Small Round Stone is the perfect size to prepare personal pizzas and smaller quantities of food for smaller families.

Inside-Out Lasagna

Lasagna gets turned upside down! Bow tie pasta is placed on the bottom of the Rectangular Baker, and seasoned ground beef and ricotta cheese follow suit.

1 **package (12 ounces) uncooked bow tie pasta**

1/2 **medium onion, chopped**

1¼ **pounds 95% lean ground beef or Italian sausage links, casings removed**

2 **garlic cloves, pressed**

1 **jar (26 ounces) marinara sauce**

1 **can (14.5 ounces) diced tomatoes in juice**

4 **eggs**

1 **container (32 ounces) part-skim ricotta cheese**

2 **cups (8 ounces) shredded mozzarella cheese**

1/2 **cup (2 ounces) grated fresh Parmesan cheese**

2 **tablespoons snipped fresh parsley**

1/2 **teaspoon salt**

1/2 **teaspoon ground black pepper**

1. Preheat oven to 350°F. Cook pasta according to package directions in **Professional (8-qt.) Stockpot**; drain.

2. Meanwhile, chop onion using **Food Chopper**. Place onion and ground beef in **Family (12-in.) Skillet**. Cook and stir over medium heat 8-10 minutes or until beef is no longer pink, breaking beef into small crumbles. Press garlic into beef mixture using **Garlic Press**. Stir in pasta sauce and tomatoes; remove from heat.

3. In **Stainless (2-qt.) Mixing Bowl**, lightly beat eggs with **Stainless Whisk**. Add cheeses, parsley, salt and black pepper; mix well.

4. To assemble lasagna, place cooked pasta into bottom of **Rectangular Baker**. Top with meat mixture. Spoon ricotta mixture over sauce; spread evenly. Bake, uncovered, 1 hour or until ricotta mixture is set and lightly browned.

Yield: 15 servings

Nutrients per serving: Calories 340, Total Fat 15 g, Saturated Fat 8 g, Cholesterol 120 mg, Carbohydrate 27 g, Protein 25 g, Sodium 740 mg, Fiber 2 g

Diabetic exchanges per serving: 1½ starch, 3 medium-fat meat (1½ carb)

cook's tips

A combination of ground beef and Italian sausage links (casings removed), can be used in this recipe, if desired.

This recipe can be prepared one day in advance. Prepare recipe through Step 4; do not bake. Cover; refrigerate overnight. When ready to bake, remove from refrigerator; let stand at room temperature 30 minutes. Bake, uncovered, 1 hour, 15 minutes or until lightly browned and edges are bubbly.

Jamaican Pork Tenderloin

Save one for later! You'll thank yourself when preparing Islander's Salad *using leftover pork tenderloin from tonight's dinner.*

PREP TIME: 25 MINUTES   COOK TIME: 25-30 MINUTES   STAND TIME: 10 MINUTES

Pork Tenderloins

- 2 pork tenderloins (about 1 pound each)
- 4 teaspoons chili powder
- 1 tablespoon salt
- 2 teaspoons ground cinnamon
- 1/4 teaspoon cayenne pepper

Apples and Vegetables

- 2 medium Braeburn or Granny Smith apples, cored and cut crosswise
- 2 large sweet potatoes (1-1 1/4 pounds), peeled and cut into 1-inch wedges
- 1 large yellow onion, cut into 1-inch wedges
- 1 tablespoon olive oil
- 1/4 cup maple-flavored syrup

1. Preheat oven to 425°F. Place pork tenderloins side by side but not touching on **Stoneware Bar Pan**. Combine chili powder, salt, cinnamon and cayenne pepper in **Prep Bowl**. Rub 2 tablespoons of the seasoning mixture over entire surface of tenderloins. Reserve remaining seasoning mixture.

2. For apples and vegetables, core apples with **The Corer™**. Cut apples crosswise in half using **Chef's Knife**. Slice sweet potatoes and onion into 1-inch wedges. Combine oil and remaining seasoning mixture in **Stainless (6-qt.) Mixing Bowl**; mix well. Add apples and vegetables; toss to coat using **Mix 'N Scraper®**.

3. Place apples and vegetables in pan surrounding tenderloins. Bake 25-30 minutes for medium (160°F) to well (170°F) doneness. Remove from oven; tent with aluminum foil and let stand 10 minutes.

4. Wrap and refrigerate one tenderloin for up to 4 days for later use in *Islander's Salad*. Carefully pour off pan juices to measure 1/4 cup. Add maple-flavored syrup; mix well. Carve remaining tenderloin into thin slices using **Carving Set**. Arrange tenderloin slices, apples and vegetables on serving platter. Serve with pan juices.

Yield: 4 servings

| LIGHT | Nutrients per serving: Calories 360, Total Fat 9 g, Saturated Fat 2.5 g, Cholesterol 65 mg, Carbohydrate 47 g, Protein 25 g, Sodium 990 mg, Fiber 7 g |

Diabetic exchanges per serving: 2 starch, 1/2 fruit, 3 low-fat meat (2 1/2 carb)

Save one cooked pork tenderloin for another day to make this recipe:

Islander's Salad
(p. 39)

Cook's Tips:

Check the internal temperature of the meat after 25 minutes of roasting to be sure it doesn't become overcooked.

Be sure to remove the "silver skin" from pork tenderloin before cooking. Silver skin is the membrane sometimes left on the pork tenderloin after the fat has been removed. To remove the membrane, slip the tip of the **Utility Knife** between the skin and the meat and lift slightly as you slice it off.

Islander's Salad

With the help of planned-over pork tenderloin, the ingredients in this vibrant, healthful salad will go from refrigerator to table in just 15 minutes.

PREP TIME: 15 MINUTES

3/4-1 **pound reserved cooked tenderloin from *Jamaican Pork Tenderloin* (p. 37)**

1 **mango, peeled and cut into 1/2-inch cubes (1 cup)**

1/2 **small red onion, sliced into thin wedges**

1 **package (6 ounces) fresh baby spinach leaves**

1 **cup fresh green beans, blanched and cut into 2-inch pieces**

1/4 **cup toasted sliced almonds (optional)**

1/4 **cup reduced-fat raspberry vinaigrette salad dressing**

1. Cut tenderloin into thin slices using **Carving Set**. Peel mango and cut into into 1/2-inch cubes using **Utility Knife**. Slice onion into thin wedges.

2. Place spinach on serving platter. Top with mango, onion, green beans and pork. Sprinkle with almonds, if desired. Serve with salad dressing.

Yield: 4 servings

| LIGHT | Nutrients per serving: Calories 230, Total Fat 7 g, Saturated Fat 2 g, Cholesterol 65 mg, Carbohydrate 17 g, Protein 25 g, Sodium 1100 mg, Fiber 3 g |

Diabetic exchanges per serving: 1/2 fruit, 1 vegetable, 3 low-fat meat (1/2 carb)

minutes or less

To peel and cube a mango, cut thin slices from both ends of the fruit. Peel from top to bottom using **Vegetable Peeler**. Stand fruit upright, stem end down, on **Cutting Board**. Carefully slice flesh alongside the large, flat pit and cut into cubes.

If desired, 1 cup cubed fresh peaches or nectarines can be substituted for the mango.

To toast almonds in the microwave oven, refer to the Cook's Tip on p. 25.

To blanch green beans, simply place them in boiling water for several seconds, then remove them with **Nylon Slotted Spoon** and immediately plunge them into ice-cold water.

Barbecue Beef Brisket

One beef brisket can create three distinctively different meals. Start here for a savory Sunday supper, then make sandwiches and stew later in the week.

PREP TIME: 15 MINUTES   COOK TIME: 2 HOURS, 30 MINUTES TO 3 HOURS   STAND TIME: 10 MINUTES

- 1 **beef brisket (5-6 pounds)**
- 4 **garlic cloves, pressed**
- 1 **teaspoon salt**
- 1/4 **teaspoon ground black pepper**
- 1 1/2 **cups ketchup**
- 1/3 **cup cider vinegar**
- 1/4 **cup brown sugar**
- 1/4 **cup Worcestershire sauce**
- 2 **tablespoons yellow mustard**
- 2 **large onions, sliced**

1. Preheat oven to 350°F. Trim excess fat from brisket and place fat side up in **Rectangular Baker**. Press garlic over brisket using **Garlic Press**, spreading evenly. Sprinkle with salt and black pepper.

2. In **Small Batter Bowl**, combine ketchup, vinegar, brown sugar, Worcestershire sauce and mustard. Pour over brisket.

3. Slice onions using **Ultimate Slice & Grate** fitted with v-shaped blade. Arrange onions over brisket. Cover baker with **Rectangular Lid/Bowl** or aluminum foil. Bake brisket 2 hours, 30 minutes to 3 hours or until fork-tender. Carefully remove lid/bowl, lifting away from you. Remove onions and brisket to **Reversible Bamboo Cutting Board**; let stand 10 minutes. Pour pan juices into **Easy Read Measuring Cup**; skim off fat from pan juices. Reserve 1 cup pan juices.

4. Slice brisket thinly across the grain (the direction the meat fibers are running) using **Carving Knife**. Wrap and refrigerate half of the onions (about 1 cup), half of the meat (about 24-32 ounces) and all remaining pan juices to be used separately for *Barbecue Beef & Peppers Sub* and *Quick Barbecue Beef Stew*.

5. Place remaining meat and onions on serving platter. Serve with 1 cup reserved pan juices.

Yield: 6-8 servings

Nutrients per serving: Calories 420, Total Fat 25 g, Saturated Fat 10 g, Cholesterol 115 mg, Carbohydrate 15 g, Protein 34 g, Sodium 640 mg, Fiber less than 1 g

Diabetic exchanges per serving: 1 fruit, 5 medium-fat meat (1 carb)

Save half of the cooked brisket for another day to make these recipes:

Barbecue Beef & Peppers Sub (p. 43)

Quick Barbecue Beef Stew (p. 45)

Cook's Tip:

If you are unable to find a beef brisket weighing 5-6 pounds, you can buy two smaller briskets weighing 2 1/2-3 pounds each. Proceed as recipe directs.

Main Dishes & More 41

Barbecue Beef & Peppers Sub

Turn last night's brisket into a saucy, flavorful sandwich for dinner tonight.

PREP AND COOK TIME: 15 MINUTES   BAKE TIME: 5-7 MINUTES

1 loaf (1 pound) Italian bread (about 17 inches long)

1 large green bell pepper, cut into 1/2-inch strips

1 large red bell pepper, cut into 1/2-inch strips

1 teaspoon vegetable oil

1/2 cup pan juices from *Barbecue Beef Brisket* (p. 41)

1 teaspoon cornstarch

3/4-1 pound cooked beef brisket (about 2 cups slices) from *Barbecue Beef Brisket*

1 cup onions from *Barbecue Beef Brisket*

8 slices (1 ounce each) Colby & Monterey Jack cheese blend

1. Preheat oven to 350°F. Cut bread in half horizontally, end to end, using **Serrated Bread Knife**. Carefully pull out sections of bread from interior of each bread half, leaving a 1/2-inch-thick bread shell, and set aside bread interior for another use (see Cook's Tip).

2. Cut bell peppers into 1/2-inch strips using **Chef's Knife**. Heat oil in **Small (8-in.) Sauté Pan** over medium heat. Add bell pepper strips and cook 6-8 minutes or until peppers are crisp-tender, stirring occasionally. Remove from heat; remove peppers from pan and set aside.

3. Discard any solidified fat from pan juices. Combine pan juices and cornstarch in same pan; whisk until smooth using **Nylon Spiral Whisk**. Bring to a boil over medium heat, stirring constantly. Reduce heat; simmer 1 minute. Add brisket slices and onions; bring to a boil. Reduce heat; simmer over low heat 5 minutes or until heated through.

4. To assemble sandwich, place bottom half of bread on **Stoneware Bar Pan**. Spoon brisket mixture over bottom half of bread. Top evenly with bell peppers, cheese and top half of bread. Bake 5-7 minutes or until heated through and cheese is melted. Cut sandwich into slices and serve.

Yield: 6 servings

Nutrients per serving: Calories 450, Total Fat 20 g, Saturated Fat 10 g, Cholesterol 75 mg, Carbohydrate 42 g, Protein 26 g, Sodium 810 mg, Fiber 2 g

Diabetic exchanges per serving: 2½ starch, 1 vegetable, 2½ medium-fat meat, 1 fat (2½ carb)

30 minutes or less

Don't throw that extra bread away! The soft bread that is pulled out of the loaves can be cubed and toasted for croutons or stuffing or grated to make bread crumbs.

Both bell and hot peppers are native to the tropical areas of the Western Hemisphere and quickly became popular in Spanish cuisine when Christopher Columbus took them back to his homeland.

When shopping for bell peppers, choose peppers that are firm and heavy for their size. Avoid peppers that are shriveled or have sunken spots. Store bell peppers in a plastic bag in the refrigerator for up to 1 week.

Quick Barbecue Beef Stew

*Planned-over beef brisket makes comforting, home-style stew
quick and easy to prepare.*

PREP TIME: 15 MINUTES   COOK TIME: 5-6 MINUTES   BAKE TIME: 14-17 MINUTES

4 **refrigerated buttermilk biscuits**

3/4-1 **pound cooked beef brisket (about
2 cups slices) from** *Barbecue Beef
Brisket* **(p. 41)**

1 **cup pan juices from** *Barbecue Beef
Brisket*

2 **tablespoons cornstarch**

1 **cup water**

2 **cups frozen petite mixed vegetable
blend (such as baby carrots, green
beans, peas and corn)**

1/2 **teaspoon dried thyme leaves**

1. Preheat oven to 350°F. Bake biscuits
   according to package directions on **Small
   Round Stone**. Meanwhile, cut brisket slices
   into 1-inch pieces using **Utility Knife**; set
   aside.

2. Discard any solidified fat from pan juices.
   Combine cornstarch, pan juices and water in
   Medium (3-qt.) Saucepan; whisk until
   smooth using **Nylon Spiral Whisk**. Bring to
   a boil over medium heat, stirring constantly.
   Reduce heat; simmer 1 minute.

3. Add brisket pieces, vegetables and thyme;
   bring to a boil. Reduce heat to low; simmer,
   uncovered, 5-6 minutes or until sauce
   thickens and vegetables are tender. Split
   biscuits; place bottoms of biscuits into serving
   bowls. Ladle 1 cup stew over each biscuit
   using **Nylon Ladle**. Place tops of biscuits
   over stew.

Yield: 4 servings

Nutrients per serving: Calories 570, Total Fat 22 g, Saturated
Fat 8 g, Cholesterol 90 mg, Carbohydrate 63 g, Protein 34 g,
Sodium 780 mg, Fiber 5 g

Diabetic exchanges per serving: 2 1/2 starch, 1 vegetable,
2 1/2 medium-fat meat, 1 fat (2 1/2 carb)

cook's tips

minutes or less

If you do not have
enough pan juices, add
enough beef broth or
water to measure 1 cup.
Use our **Easy Read
Measuring Cups** to give
you the perfect
measurement.

Refrigerated buttermilk
biscuits can be found
near the refrigerated
crescent roll dough in
most supermarkets.
You can also find
portioned biscuits in the
freezer section of your
supermarket. Thaw and
bake according to
package directions.

If desired, any of
your favorite frozen
vegetable blends can be
substituted for the petite
mixed vegetable blend.

Spicy Oven-Fried Cod Fillets

After enjoying these light, flavorful fillets and zesty sauce, your family will agree that the traditional fish fry is a thing of the past.

PREP TIME: 10 MINUTES   BAKE TIME: 15-18 MINUTES

Sauce

- 2 teaspoons thinly sliced green onion with top
- 1 small garlic clove, pressed
- 1/2 cup reduced-fat Thousand Island salad dressing
- 1/4 teaspoon chili powder
  Dash cayenne pepper

Cod Fillets

- 1 egg, lightly beaten
- 1/2 cup dry Italian-style bread crumbs
- 1/4 teaspoon chili powder
- 1/4 teaspoon salt
- 1 1/2 pounds cod fish fillets (about 4 fillets)

1. Preheat oven to 450°F. For sauce, thinly slice green onion with **Chef's Knife**. Press garlic into **Prep Bowl** using **Garlic Press**. Add onion, salad dressing, chili powder and cayenne pepper; mix well. Cover; refrigerate at least 1 hour to allow flavors to blend.

2. For cod fillets, lightly beat egg in **Small Batter Bowl** using **Stainless Mini Whisk**. Combine bread crumbs, chili powder and salt in shallow dish. Dip fillets into egg, then into bread crumb mixture, coating evenly. Arrange fillets on **Medium Bar Pan**; lightly spray with nonstick cooking spray.

3. Bake 15-18 minutes or until cod flakes easily with a fork. Remove from oven; serve cod with sauce.

Yield: 4 servings

LIGHT   Nutrients per serving: Calories 270, Total Fat 5 g, Saturated Fat .5 g, Cholesterol 125 mg, Carbohydrate 20 g, Protein 33 g, Sodium 960 mg, Fiber less than 1 g

Diabetic exchanges per serving: 1 starch, 4 low-fat meat (1 carb)

30 minutes or less

Cod is a popular saltwater fish with mild-flavored, firm meat. If desired, any firm, white fish fillets such as red snapper or whitefish (about 6 ounces each) can be substituted for the cod fillets.

Cod fillets vary in size, so you may need to cut fillets to form the number of servings you desire.

The tangy, spicy sauce that accompanies this dish is a spin-off from traditional tartar sauce, which is made with mayonnaise, dill or sweet pickles, lemon juice and sometimes capers. This sauce is similar to French *rémoulade*, which is also mayonnaise-based and includes mustard, capers and chopped gherkin pickles.

Roasting vegetables intensifies flavor by using high heat and allowing the natural sugars in the vegetables to caramelize. Make sure not to crowd the pan or the vegetables will steam rather than roast.

For variety, create a medley of roasted vegetables by combining two or three vegetables from the chart that have the same roasting time.

After roasting, try adding in snipped fresh herbs such as basil, oregano, parsley or chives. For heightened flavor, add a splash of balsamic vinegar.

Present your favorite selection of roasted vegetables on a large platter for a simple and colorful appetizer. Serve at room temperature with assorted cheeses and fresh crusty bread.

Roasted Vegetables

This helpful chart will provide simple instructions for preparing and roasting all of your favorite vegetables. Mix and match them as we have done in our Roasted Vegetable Focaccia Sandwich *(p. 51),* Harvest Cream Soup *(p. 53) and* Mediterranean Orzo Salad *(p. 55).*

1. Preheat oven to 450°F. Prepare vegetables as directed below. Toss prepared vegetables in 1-2 tablespoons olive oil and garlic pressed with **Garlic Press**.

2. Arrange vegetables in a single layer on **Stoneware Bar Pan** (do not crowd pan); season with salt and coarsely ground black pepper, if desired.

3. Roast vegetables according to time indicated in chart or until tender, deep golden brown and beginning to caramelize.

Vegetable	Preparation	Roasting Time
Asparagus	Cut off woody ends.	25-30 minutes
Bell Peppers	Cut into 1-inch strips.	25-30 minutes
Cauliflower	Cut into florets.	25-30 minutes
Eggplant	Cut into 1/4-inch slices.	25-30 minutes
Mushrooms	Trim off stem ends.	25-30 minutes
Plum Tomatoes	Cut in half.	25-30 minutes
Red or Yellow Onions	Cut into 1/2-inch wedges or slices.	25-30 minutes
Yellow Summer Squash or Zucchini	Cut into 1/4-inch slices.	25-30 minutes
New Potatoes	Do not peel; cut in half.	30-35 minutes
Russet, Yukon Gold or Sweet Potatoes	Do not peel; cut into 1/2-inch slices.	30-35 minutes
Baby Carrots	Leave whole.	40-45 minutes
Carrots	Cut into 1/2-inch slices.	40-45 minutes
Leeks	Cut in half lengthwise, then into 2-inch pieces.	40-45 minutes
Squash, such as Butternut or Acorn	Peel and cut into 1-inch cubes.	40-45 minutes

Roasted Vegetable Focaccia Sandwich

This fresh vegetable sandwich is beautiful to behold and is the perfect take-along for a picnic dinner.

PREP TIME: 15 MINUTES   BAKE TIME: 25-30 MINUTES   COOL TIME: 15 MINUTES

1   medium eggplant

1   large zucchini

1   tablespoon olive oil

2   garlic cloves, pressed

Salt and coarsely ground black pepper (optional)

2   balls fresh mozzarella cheese (8 ounces), sliced

1   medium tomato, sliced

1   (7 1/2-inch) loaf focaccia bread (about 12 ounces)

1/4   cup reduced-fat mayonnaise

1/2   cup loosely packed fresh basil leaves

1. Preheat oven to 450°F. Cut eggplant and zucchini crosswise into 1/4-inch-thick slices using **Chef's Knife**. Combine eggplant, zucchini and oil in **Stainless (6-qt.) Mixing Bowl**. Press garlic into mixing bowl using **Garlic Press**; toss to coat using **Mix 'N Scraper®**. Season with salt and black pepper, if desired.

2. Arrange vegetables in a single layer on **Stoneware Bar Pan**. Bake 25-30 minutes or until vegetables are tender and deep golden brown. Remove from oven to **Stackable Cooling Rack**; cool slightly.

3. Meanwhile, cut mozzarella and tomato into 1/4-inch-thick slices. Cut bread in half horizontally using **Serrated Bread Knife**. Spread mayonnaise on cut surfaces using **Small Spreader**.

4. To assemble sandwich, arrange basil leaves, vegetables, tomato slices and mozzarella slices over bottom half of bread. Top with top half of bread. Cut into slices and serve.

Yield: 6 servings

Nutrients per serving: Calories 460, Total Fat 24 g, Saturated Fat 12 g, Cholesterol 65 mg, Carbohydrate 42 g, Protein 19 g, Sodium 510 mg, Fiber 5 g

Diabetic exchanges per serving: 2 1/2 starch, 2 high-fat meat, 1 1/2 fat (2 1/2 carb)

Pantry Basil Oil can be substituted for the olive oil, if desired.

Substitute 1 large yellow squash, cut diagonally into 1/4-inch-thick slices or 2 large red, green or yellow bell peppers, cut into 1-inch-thick strips for the eggplant or zucchini, if desired.

Fresh mozzarella cheese has a soft, spongy texture and mild, slightly sweet flavor. It plays a key role in popular caprese salad, comprising slices of fresh mozzarella, tomatoes and basil leaves drizzled with olive oil. Fresh mozzarella is shaped in small or large balls packaged in whey or water and can be found in Italian specialty markets, as well as the deli or cheese section of most grocery stores.

Harvest Cream Soup

This upscale pureed soup, finished with a splash of fresh ginger juice and a swirl of sour cream, is remarkably easy to make.

PREP TIME: 15 MINUTES BAKE TIME: 40-45 MINUTES COOK TIME: 10 MINUTES

1 **butternut squash (1 pound)**

2 **large leeks (white and light green portions only)**

1 **pound baby carrots (about 3 cups)**

1 **tablespoon olive oil**

1 **garlic clove, pressed**

   Salt and coarsely ground black pepper (optional)

2 **cans (14-14$^{1}/_{2}$ ounces each) 99% fat-free chicken broth, divided**

1 **can (12 ounces) evaporated whole milk**

1 **1-inch piece unpeeled fresh gingerroot, grated and juiced**

   Reduced-fat sour cream (optional)

1. Preheat oven to 450°F. Cut squash into 1-inch pieces. Cut leeks in half lengthwise, then into 2-inch pieces. Combine squash, leeks, carrots and oil in **Stainless (6-qt.) Mixing Bowl**. Press garlic into mixing bowl with **Garlic Press**; toss to coat using **Mix 'N Scraper®**. Season with salt and black pepper, if desired.

2. Arrange vegetables in a single layer on **Stoneware Bar Pan**. Bake 40-45 minutes or until vegetables are tender and deep golden brown. Remove from oven to **Stackable Cooling Rack**.

3. Combine half of the vegetables with one can of the chicken broth in blender or food processor container. Cover; blend until smooth. Pour mixture into **Professional (4-qt.) Casserole**. Repeat with remaining vegetable mixture and chicken broth. Add evaporated milk to casserole. Cook over medium heat 5-6 minutes or until heated through, stirring occasionally.

4. Grate gingerroot using **Ultimate Slice & Grate**. Gather gingerroot in palm of hand and squeeze over **Prep Bowl** to yield 2 teaspoons juice; discard flesh. Stir juice into soup just before serving. Season to taste with salt and black pepper. Ladle soup into bowls; swirl in sour cream, if desired.

Yield: 6 servings (about 7$^{1}/_{2}$ cups)

Nutrients per serving: Calories 180, Total Fat 8 g, Saturated Fat 3 g, Cholesterol 20 mg, Carbohydrate 24 g, Protein 6 g, Sodium 910 mg, Fiber 4 g

Diabetic exchanges per serving: 1 starch, 1 vegetable, 1$^{1}/_{2}$ fat (1 carb)

To clean leeks, cut in half lengthwise and rinse thoroughly to remove all of the sand and grit.

The white and light green parts of leeks are the most tender portions. Do not use the dark green leaves.

To reduce fat and calories, substitute evaporated 2% milk or evaporated fat-free milk for the evaporated whole milk.

To swirl sour cream into serving bowls, drop several dollops by teaspoon into each bowl. Carefully drag the **Cake Tester** through dollops to make pretty designs.

Mediterranean Orzo Salad

Fresh, colorful and delicious, this meatless pasta salad is a meal in itself or can be used as a hearty side dish.

PREP TIME: 20 MINUTES   BAKE TIME: 25-30 MINUTES   COOL TIME: 30 MINUTES

1   **pound asparagus spears, trimmed**
1   **large red bell pepper, cut into 1-inch wedges**
1   **medium red onion, sliced into 1/2-inch wedges**
1   **tablespoon olive oil**
2   **garlic cloves, pressed**
    Salt and coarsely ground black pepper (optional)
3/4 **cup uncooked orzo pasta**
1   **can (15 ounces) garbanzo beans, drained and rinsed**
1   **package (4 ounces) crumbled feta cheese**
1/2 **cup pitted whole kalamata olives**
1/4 **cup snipped fresh parsley**
1/4 **cup prepared Greek vinaigrette dressing**
    Romaine lettuce leaves (optional)

1. Preheat oven to 450°F. Combine asparagus, bell pepper, onion and oil in **Stainless (6-qt.) Mixing Bowl**. Press garlic into mixing bowl using **Garlic Press**; toss to coat using **Mix 'N Scraper®**. Season with salt and black pepper, if desired.

2. Arrange vegetables in a single layer on **Stoneware Bar Pan**. Bake 25-30 minutes or until vegetables are tender and deep golden brown. Remove from oven to **Stackable Cooling Rack**; cool completely. Cut asparagus and bell pepper into 1-inch pieces.

3. Meanwhile, prepare orzo according to package directions in **Small (2-qt.) Saucepan**; drain and rinse under cold running water in small **Colander**. Place orzo in **Stainless (4-qt.) Mixing Bowl**. Add vegetable mixture, beans, feta cheese, olives, parsley and salad dressing; toss gently. Serve at room temperature or cover and refrigerate until ready to serve. Serve over lettuce leaves, if desired.

Yield: 4 servings

Nutrients per serving: Calories 460, Total Fat 21 g, Saturated Fat 6 g, Cholesterol 25 mg, Carbohydrate 55 g, Protein 16 g, Sodium 980 mg, Fiber 8 g

Diabetic exchanges per serving: 3 starch, 1 medium-fat meat, 3 fat (3 carb)

Vegetables can be roasted up to 2 hours ahead. Let stand at room temperature until you're ready to use them.

Orzo is a tiny, rice-shaped pasta, which can be found in the pasta section of most grocery stores.

To trim asparagus, snap off and discard tough stem ends.

Italian dressing can be substituted for the Greek vinaigrette dressing, if desired.

Lemon Greek Chicken

This hearty one-dish meal tastes like it's straight from the Mediterranean. Pass a loaf of warm, crusty bread, and there will be no end to the compliments you'll receive.

PREP TIME: 20 MINUTES   BAKE TIME: 1 HOUR

2   lemons, divided

1/4   cup olive oil

4   large garlic cloves, pressed

2-3 teaspoons dried oregano leaves

3/4   teaspoon salt

1/2   teaspoon coarsely ground black
       pepper

4   split (bone-in) chicken breast halves
       (2 1/2-3 pounds)

8   petite red potatoes (about
       12 ounces)

1   medium red bell pepper, cut into
       1-inch strips

1   medium red onion, cut into
       1-inch wedges

8   ounces whole mushrooms

1. Preheat oven to 400°F. Using **Lemon Zester/Scorer**, zest one lemon to measure 1 1/2 tablespoons zest. Juice lemon using **Juicer** to measure 2 tablespoons juice. In **Stainless (4-qt.) Mixing Bowl**, combine lemon zest, juice, oil, garlic pressed with **Garlic Press**, oregano, salt and black pepper; mix well.

2. Place chicken on center of **Stoneware Bar Pan**. Using **Pastry Brush**, brush chicken with a portion of the lemon juice mixture.

3. Using **Crinkle Cutter**, cut potatoes in half. Using **Utility Knife**, cut bell pepper into 1-inch strips; cut strips in half. Cut onion into 1-inch wedges. Thinly slice remaining lemon. Combine potatoes, bell pepper, onion, lemon slices and mushrooms with remaining lemon juice mixture in mixing bowl; toss to coat.

4. Arrange vegetables around chicken on pan. Bake 1 hour or until chicken is no longer pink in center, brushing chicken and vegetables with pan juices after 30 minutes.

Yield: 4 servings

Nutrients per serving: Calories 560, Total Fat 27 g, Saturated Fat 6 g, Cholesterol 140 mg, Carbohydrate 25 g, Protein 54 g, Sodium 560 mg, Fiber 4 g

Diabetic exchanges per serving: 1 starch, 1 vegetable, 7 low-fat meat, 1 fat (1 carb)

Pantry Basil Oil can be substituted for the olive oil, if desired.

The ingredients in this recipe can be easily cut in half to serve two. Proceed as recipe directs and bake on the **Medium Bar Pan**.

It's not necessary to peel the potatoes for many recipes. Simply scrub them well and pat them dry with a paper towel before cutting them into desired shapes. With the skins left on, the potatoes retain more flavor and nutrients.

Believe it or not, oregano was rare in the United States until soldiers returning from Italy after World War II raved about it. Oregano is a member of the mint family and has an assertive flavor that awakens tomato-based dishes, poultry and meats.

Divide and save this sauce for another day to make these recipes:

Beef Tostadas

Pasta Roll-Ups (p. 61)

Chili Bread Bowls (p. 63)

Hearty Meat Sauce

This basic meat sauce is designed to be used in a variety of ways.

PREP TIME: 10 MINUTES   COOK TIME: 55-65 MINUTES

- 3 **medium onions, chopped**
- 3 **pounds 90% lean ground beef**
- 3 **garlic cloves, pressed**
- 3 **cans (28 ounces each) diced tomatoes in juice, undrained**
- 3 **cans (8 ounces each) tomato sauce**
- 1½ **tablespoons sugar**

1. Chop onions using **Food Chopper**. Heat **Family (12-in.) Skillet** over medium-high heat until hot. Add onions, ground beef and garlic pressed with **Garlic Press**. Cook 15-18 minutes or until no longer pink, breaking beef into crumbles; drain.

2. Transfer meat mixture to **Professional (8-qt.) Stockpot**. Add tomatoes, tomato sauce and sugar. Bring to a boil. Reduce heat to medium-low; simmer 40-45 minutes or until sauce thickens, stirring occasionally. Remove from heat, cool slightly.

3. Place about 5 cups sauce in separate freezer containers. Refrigerate up to 4 days or freeze up to 3 months for *Beef Tostadas, Pasta Roll-Ups* or *Chili Bread Bowls*.

Yield: 15 cups

Nutrients per serving (1 cup): Calories 220, Total Fat 9 g, Saturated Fat 3.5 g, Cholesterol 60 mg, Carbohydrate 13 g, Protein 20 g, Sodium 610 mg, Fiber 2 g

Diabetic exchanges per serving (1 cup): 1 starch, 2½ low-fat meat (1 carb)

Beef Tostadas

This recipe uses Hearty Meat Sauce in an unexpected, family-pleasing way.

30 minutes or less

PREP AND COOK TIME: 15 MINUTES   BAKE TIME: 3-4 MINUTES

- ⅓ **recipe (5 cups) prepared *Hearty Meat Sauce* (see above)**
- 1 **envelope (1 ounce) taco seasoning mix**
- 12 **(5-inch) flat corn tostada shells Desired toppings (optional)**

1. Preheat oven to 350°F. In **Medium (3-qt.) Saucepan**, combine meat sauce and seasoning mix. Bring to a boil; reduce heat to medium-low and simmer 10 minutes.

2. Meanwhile, place six tostada shells on **Large Round Stone**. Bake shells 3-4 minutes or until crisp. Repeat with remaining shells.

3. Place two shells on each serving plate. Divide meat sauce evenly among shells; top with desired toppings.

Yield: 6 servings

Nutrients per serving (2 tostadas): Calories 320, Total Fat 14 g, Saturated Fat 4 g, Cholesterol 50 mg, Carbohydrate 31 g, Protein 18 g, Sodium 950 mg, Fiber 4 g

Diabetic exchanges per serving (2 tostadas): 2 starch, 2 medium-fat meat (2 carb)

Pasta Roll-Ups

Preparing lasagna, usually an involved, time-consuming process, is easy when planned-over meat sauce and a creative use of lasagna noodles are used.

PREP AND COOK TIME: 20 MINUTES   BAKE TIME: 40-45 MINUTES   STAND TIME: 10 MINUTES

9 uncooked lasagna noodles

1/3 recipe (5 cups) prepared *Hearty Meat Sauce* (p. 58)

1 can (8 ounces) tomato sauce

1 tablespoon *Pantry Italian Seasoning Mix*

1/3 cup (about 1 1/2 ounces) grated fresh Parmesan cheese

2 tablespoons snipped fresh parsley

1 container (15 ounces) part-skim ricotta cheese

1 egg yolk

1/4 teaspoon salt

1/8 teaspoon ground black pepper

Dash nutmeg

Additional grated fresh Parmesan cheese and snipped fresh parsley (optional)

1. Preheat oven to 350°F. Cook noodles in **Professional (8-qt.) Stockpot** according to package directions; drain. Meanwhile, combine meat sauce, tomato sauce and seasoning mix in **Medium (3-qt.) Saucepan**. Bring to a boil; reduce heat to medium-low and simmer 10 minutes.

2. Grate Parmesan cheese using **Deluxe Cheese Grater**. Snip parsley using **Kitchen Shears**. In **Classic Batter Bowl**, combine Parmesan cheese, parsley, ricotta cheese, egg yolk, salt, black pepper and nutmeg; mix until well blended.

3. Using **Large Scoop**, place 1 scoop cheese mixture on one end of each lasagna noodle; gently roll up. Spoon 3 cups of the sauce into **Square Baker**. Place roll-ups on top of sauce, seam sides down. Spoon remaining sauce over roll-ups.

4. Cover baker with aluminum foil. Bake 40-45 minutes or until sauce is bubbly. Remove baker from oven; carefully remove foil. Sprinkle with additional Parmesan cheese and parsley, if desired. Let stand 10 minutes before serving.

Yield: 9 servings

Nutrients per serving (1 roll-up): Calories 310, Total Fat 11 g, Saturated Fat 5 g, Cholesterol 80 mg, Carbohydrate 32 g, Protein 22 g, Sodium 660 mg, Fiber 2 g

Diabetic exchanges per serving (1 roll-up): 2 starch, 2 medium-fat meat (2 carb)

This recipe can be prepared as directed up to 1 day in advance. Cover baker with aluminum foil and refrigerate. When ready to bake, remove baker from refrigerator; let stand at room temperature 30 minutes. Increase baking time to 55-60 minutes; proceed as recipe directs.

Italian seasoning can be substituted for the Italian Seasoning Mix, if desired.

Nutmeg is native to the Spice Islands and is the seed of a tropical evergreen tree. It lends a complex flavor to baked goods, as well as Italian dishes and cream-based dishes such as creamed spinach.

Chili Bread Bowls

Starting with planned-over meat sauce makes preparing bread bowls and chili, in the style of bakery chains, a possible option for a weekend lunch.

PREP TIME: 10 MINUTES   BAKE TIME: 21-23 MINUTES   COOK TIME: 10 MINUTES

Bread Bowls

2 packages (13.8 ounces each) refrigerated pizza crust

1 tablespoon olive oil

1/2 cup (2 ounces) grated fresh Parmesan cheese

Chili

1/3 recipe (5 cups) prepared *Hearty Meat Sauce* (p. 58)

1 can (15 1/2 ounces) chili beans in sauce, undrained

1 envelope (1.25-1.48 ounces) chili seasoning mix

Sliced green onions with tops (optional)

1. Preheat oven to 400°F. Remove pizza crust dough from packages; do not unroll. Cut each portion of dough crosswise into thirds to form six equal portions. Place dough, cut-side down, on **Large Round Stone**; press lightly to form 4-inch rounds. Brush lightly with oil and sprinkle with Parmesan cheese. Bake 21-23 minutes or until deep golden brown. Remove from oven to **Stackable Cooling Rack**.

2. Meanwhile, in **Medium (3-qt.) Saucepan**, combine meat sauce, chili beans and seasoning mix. Bring to a boil. Reduce heat to medium-low; simmer 10 minutes.

3. To serve, slice off top of each bread round; carefully remove centers to form bowls. Place bread bowls into serving bowls; ladle chili into bread bowls. Sprinkle with green onions, if desired.

Yield: 6 servings

Nutrients per serving: Calories 670, Total Fat 18 g, Saturated Fat 5 g, Cholesterol 55 mg, Carbohydrate 88 g, Protein 35 g, Sodium 2180 mg, Fiber 9 g

Diabetic exchanges per serving: 5 starch, 3 medium-fat meat (5 carb)

Chili seasoning mix consists of chili powder, garlic powder, oregano and other spices. It can be found in the spice aisle of the grocery store near the other seasoning mix packets.

These handy, edible bowls can also be used for dips, hearty soups or stews.

Cheesy Chicken Tortellini Bake

Cubed cooked chicken and refrigerated tortellini
make a quick, comforting casserole.

PREP AND COOK TIME: 10 MINUTES   BAKE TIME: 15-20 MINUTES

Pasta Mixture

- 1/2 **cup chopped onion**
- 1 **teaspoon olive oil**
- 1 **garlic clove, pressed**
- 1 **jar (16 ounces) white Alfredo pasta sauce**
- 2 **packages (9 ounces each) refrigerated cheese-filled regular or spinach tortellini**
- 1 1/2 **cups cubed cooked chicken**
- 1 **cup milk**
- 1 **cup water**
- 1 **cup frozen peas**
- 1/4 **teaspoon ground black pepper**
- 2 **tablespoons snipped fresh basil leaves or 1 teaspoon dried basil leaves**

Crumb Topping

- 1/4 **cup (1 ounce) grated fresh Parmesan cheese**
- 2 **tablespoons butter or margarine, melted**
- 1 **cup fresh bread crumbs**

1. Preheat oven to 400°F. For pasta mixture, chop onion using **Food Chopper**. In **Professional (4-qt.) Casserole**, heat oil over medium-high heat; add onion and garlic pressed with **Garlic Press**. Cook and stir 2-3 minutes or until onion is tender. Stir in pasta sauce, tortellini, chicken, milk, water, peas and black pepper. Heat until mixture just comes to a boil; remove from heat. Stir basil into pasta mixture.

2. Meanwhile, for crumb topping, grate Parmesan cheese using **Deluxe Cheese Grater**. Place butter in **Small Micro-Cooker®**; microwave on HIGH 30-45 seconds or until melted. Stir in bread crumbs and cheese; mix well.

3. Spoon pasta mixture into **Square Baker**; sprinkle with crumb topping. Bake 15-20 minutes or until edges are bubbly and topping is golden brown.

Yield: 6 servings

Nutrients per servings: Calories 550, Total Fat 24 g, Saturated Fat 12 g, Cholesterol 110 mg, Carbohydrate 54 g, Protein 28 g, Sodium 1150 mg, Fiber 4 g

Diabetic exchanges per serving: 3 starch, 1 vegetable, 2 1/2 high-fat meat (3 carb)

cook's tips

30 minutes or less

Alfredo sauce in a jar can be found in the pasta sauce section of the supermarket. Do not substitute refrigerated Alfredo sauce; it may separate and curdle during baking.

Use the **Deluxe Cheese Grater** fitted with coarse grating drum to quickly grate bread for fresh bread crumbs.

To quickly snip basil leaves, stack the leaves and roll them up into a tight cylinder. Using the **Chef's Knife**, slice the roll crosswise into thin strips. Separate strands and snip them using **Kitchen Shears**.

Cheeseburger Stuffed Calzone

This larger-than-life calzone is like a stuffed cheeseburger pizza! Kids will enjoy the fun flavor, and you will appreciate that it is so easy to make.

PREP AND COOK TIME: 20 MINUTES   BAKE TIME: 18-20 MINUTES

1 **pound 95% lean ground beef**

1/2 **cup chopped onion**

1/4 **cup dill pickle slices, diced**

3/4 **cup ketchup**

2 **teaspoons yellow mustard**

1 **garlic clove, pressed**

2 **packages (11 ounces each) refrigerated French bread dough, divided**

6 **slices (3/4 ounce each) American pasteurized process cheese food**

1 **tablespoon olive oil**

1/4 **cup (1 ounce) grated fresh Parmesan cheese (optional)**

Optional toppings such as shredded lettuce, tomato slices, dill pickle slices, additional ketchup and mustard

1. Preheat oven to 400°F. Place ground beef in **Family (12-in.) Skillet**. Cook over medium heat 10-12 minutes or until no longer pink, breaking beef into crumbles; drain. Chop onion using **Food Chopper**. Dice pickles using **Utility Knife**. In **Classic Batter Bowl**, combine onion, pickles, ketchup, mustard and garlic pressed with **Garlic Press**; mix well. Add ground beef; mix well.

2. Unroll one package of the bread dough onto **Large Round Stone**; roll and stretch to edge of baking stone using **Baker's Roller**™. Cut cheese slices in half and arrange evenly over dough to within 1 inch of edge. Spoon meat mixture over cheese; spread evenly.

3. Unroll remaining package of dough directly over filling, matching edges of dough and shaping to fit as dough is unrolled. Trim excess dough from corners using **Pizza Cutter**, forming even edges. Roll and crimp edges to seal. Drizzle oil over dough; spread evenly. If desired, grate Parmesan cheese over dough using **Deluxe Cheese Grater**. Using Pizza Cutter, make three crisscross cuts, about 6 inches long, across center of top crust to vent. Bake 18-20 minutes or until deep golden brown. Remove from oven; cut into wedges. Serve with toppings, if desired.

Yield: 8 servings

| LIGHT | Nutrients per serving: Calories 360, Total Fat 11 g, Saturated Fat 5 g, Cholesterol 50 mg, Carbohydrate 42 g, Protein 22 g, Sodium 1060 mg, Fiber 2 g |

Diabetic exchanges per serving: 2 1/2 starch, 2 medium-fat meat, (2 1/2 carb)

Keep refrigerated French bread dough in the refrigerator until you are ready to unroll it.

Make it fun! Place toppings into **Prep Bowls** with **Bamboo Tongs** and let your little guests help themselves.

Store beef in the coldest part of the refrigerator. Ground beef can be refrigerated 1 to 2 days, and other cuts of beef can be refrigerated up to 3 days. Ground beef that is wrapped airtight can be frozen up to 3 months; solid cuts up to 6 months.

Sausage and Peppers Brunch Bake

*This hearty egg dish features zesty Italian sausage and a layer
of hash browns for a little bit of everything in each bite.*

PREP TIME: 25 MINUTES   BAKE TIME: 45-50 MINUTES   STAND TIME: 10 MINUTES

- 2 **packages (7 ounces each) frozen toaster hash brown patties, thawed (8 patties)**
- 1 **jar (12 ounces) sweet roasted red peppers, drained and patted dry**
- 1 **medium onion, chopped**
- 1 **pound hot Italian turkey sausage, casings removed**
- 6 **ounces reduced-fat cream cheese (Neufchâtel), softened**
- 3/4 **cup milk**
- 12 **eggs**
- 1 **tablespoon snipped fresh parsley**
- 1/4 **teaspoon ground black pepper**

1. Preheat oven to 350°F. Spray **Rectangular Baker** with nonstick cooking spray. Arrange hash brown patties in a single layer over bottom of baker. Dice red peppers using **Chef's Knife**. Chop onion using **Food Chopper**. In **Family (12-in.) Skillet**, cook and stir sausage and onion over medium heat 8-10 minutes or until sausage is no longer pink, breaking sausage into crumbles; drain.

2. In **Classic Batter Bowl**, whisk cream cheese and milk until completely smooth using **Stainless Whisk**. Add eggs, parsley and black pepper; whisk until smooth.

3. Spoon sausage mixture evenly over hash browns; sprinkle with red peppers. Pour egg mixture over peppers. Bake 45-50 minutes or until center of egg mixture is set. Remove from oven; let stand 10 minutes. Cut into squares and serve using **Large Serving Spatula**.

Yield: 15 servings

Nutrients per serving: Calories 210, Total Fat 13 g, Saturated Fat 5 g, Cholesterol 195 mg, Carbohydrate 11 g, Protein 12 g, Sodium 430 mg, Fiber less than 1 g

Diabetic exchanges per serving: 1 starch, 1 medium-fat meat, 1 fat (1 carb)

cook's tips

One package (16 ounces) uncooked breakfast sausage, casings removed, can be substituted for the Italian turkey sausage, if desired.

This recipe can be prepared up to 1 day ahead. Prepare recipe as directed. Refrigerate, covered, overnight. When ready to serve, preheat oven to 325°F. Uncover baker; bake 55 minutes-1 hour or until egg mixture is set.

Woven Selections™ rattan pieces are beautifully designed to fit our Stoneware pieces.

something
sweet

If it's your turn to bring dessert, have no fear. This array of tempting desserts and treats is sure to steal the show.

Berries 'N Stars (p. 72)

Berries 'N Stars

For a star-spangled finale, serve this beautiful, fruit-filled pastry. Garnish it with elegant swirls of whipped topping using our Easy Accent® Decorator.

PREP TIME: 30 MINUTES   BAKE TIME: 15-18 MINUTES   COOL TIME: 1 HOUR

1 **package (17.25 ounces) frozen puff pastry sheets, thawed**

2 **lemons**

1 **can (14 ounces) sweetened condensed milk (not evaporated milk)**

1 **container (8 ounces) frozen whipped topping, thawed**

1 **quart strawberries, hulled and sliced (about 3 cups slices)**

1/2 **pint blueberries (about 1 cup)**
   Powdered sugar

1. Preheat oven to 400°F. Unfold one pastry sheet onto lightly floured **Rectangle Stone**. Roll into a 13 x 10-inch rectangle using lightly floured **Baker's Roller™**. Move pastry into one corner of the stone, leaving open space along two sides. Unfold second sheet of pastry onto smooth side of **Large Grooved Cutting Board**; roll into a 13 x 10-inch rectangle. Cut four 1-inch-thick strips lengthwise from second sheet using **Pizza Cutter**; reserve remaining dough for decoration. Brush outer edges of pastry on baking stone with water using **Pastry Brush**. Arrange and press strips around edge of pastry, forming an even border. Trim off any excess dough. Prick entire bottom of pastry with pastry tool.

2. Cut 16 stars from remaining sheet of dough using **Creative Cutters** (discard remaining dough). Arrange stars in space along edges of baking stone. Bake 15-18 minutes or until golden brown. (Center of crust may puff up slightly, but will flatten out as it cools.) Cool completely. Remove pastry stars from baking stone; set aside.

3. Meanwhile, zest lemons with **Microplane® Adjustable Grater** to measure 1 tablespoon zest. Juice lemons using **Juicer** to measure 1/4 cup juice. In **Classic Batter Bowl**, whisk together condensed milk, lemon zest and juice using **Stainless Whisk**. Gently fold in whipped topping using **Classic Scraper**. Attach desired tip to **Easy Accent® Decorator**; completely fill with filling mixture (1 1/3 cups) and set aside for garnish.

4. Fill cooled pastry shell within border with remaining filling. Hull strawberries using **Cook's Corer™**; slice using **Egg Slicer Plus®**. Arrange strawberries and blueberries over filling. Garnish with rosettes of reserved filling and pastry stars. Refrigerate until ready to serve. Lightly sprinkle pastry with powdered sugar using **Flour/Sugar Shaker**. Slice using **Chef's Knife**.

Yield: 16 servings

Nutrients per serving: Calories 290, Total Fat 13 g, Saturated Fat 6 g, Cholesterol 10 mg, Carbohydrate 40 g, Protein 5 g, Sodium 135 mg, Fiber 4 g

Diabetic exchanges per serving: 2 starch, 1/2 fruit, 2 fat (2 1/2 carb)

Blueberry-Almond Oat Muffins

When filling the bread basket at your next brunch, be sure to try all three delicious varieties of muffins that are offered here!

PREP TIME: 15 MINUTES   BAKE TIME: 18-20 MINUTES

cook's tips

1½ **cups all-purpose flour**
1 **cup quick rolled oats**
¾ **cup packed brown sugar**
1 **tablespoon baking powder**
¼ **teaspoon salt**
1 **cup blueberries**
1 **tablespoon lemon zest**
1 **cup milk**
¼ **cup butter or margarine, melted**
1 **egg, lightly beaten**
¼ **cup sliced almonds, coarsely chopped**
  Powdered sugar (optional)

1. Preheat oven to 425°F. Spray **Stoneware Muffin Pan** with nonstick cooking spray or line with paper liners.

2. Combine flour, oats, brown sugar, baking powder and salt in **Stainless (2-qt.) Mixing Bowl**; mix well. Stir in blueberries and lemon zest. Add milk, butter and egg; mix just until dry ingredients are moistened.

3. Using **Large Scoop**, scoop batter into muffin cups. Sprinkle almonds evenly over batter, pressing down gently. Bake 18-20 minutes or until golden brown. Remove from oven to **Stackable Cooling Rack**. Cool 5 minutes; remove from pan. Sprinkle powdered sugar over muffins using **Flour/Sugar Shaker**, if desired. Serve warm.

Yield: 12 muffins

LIGHT Nutrients per serving: Calories 200, Total Fat 6 g, Saturated Fat 3 g, Cholesterol 30 mg, Carbohydrate 33 g, Protein 4 g, Sodium 220 mg, Fiber 2 g

Diabetic exchanges per serving: 2 starch, 1 fat (2 carb)

Variations: *Carrot-Raisin Oat Muffins:* Omit almonds. Add 1 teaspoon **Pantry Cinnamon Plus Spice Blend** to dry ingredients. Substitute ⅔ cup shredded carrots and ⅓ cup raisins for the blueberries and omit lemon zest. Combine ingredients and scoop batter into muffin cups as directed in Steps 2 and 3. Using **Small Scoop**, place one rounded scoop of plain soft cream cheese or pineapple soft cream cheese spread on top of batter in each muffin cup. Top with pecan half, if desired. Bake as directed above.

Nutrients per serving: Calories 250, Total Fat 10 g, Saturated Fat 6 g, Cholesterol 45 mg, Carbohydrate 35 g, Protein 5 g, Sodium 270 mg, Fiber 2 g

Diabetic exchanges per serving: 2 starch, 2 fat (2 carb)

Dutch Apple Oat Muffins: Omit almonds. Add 1 teaspoon **Pantry Korintje Cinnamon** to dry ingredients. Substitute 1 cup chopped apple for the blueberries and omit lemon zest. Combine ingredients and scoop into muffin cups as directed in Steps 2 and 3. For streusel, combine ¼ cup each flour, oats and brown sugar and 3 tablespoons melted butter or margarine; mix well. Sprinkle streusel evenly over batter in each muffin cup. Bake as directed above.

LIGHT Nutrients per serving: Calories 250, Total Fat 8 g, Saturated Fat 4.5 g, Cholesterol 35 mg, Carbohydrate 40 mg, Protein 4 g, Sodium 240 mg, Fiber 2 g

Diabetic exchanges per serving: 1 starch, 1½ fruit, 1½ fat (2½ carb)

Pumpkin pie spice can be substituted for the Cinnamon Plus Spice Blend and ground cinnamon can be substituted for the Korintje Cinnamon, if desired.

To freeze *Blueberry-Almond Oat Muffins* and *Dutch Apple Oat Muffins*, cool completely after baking. Place in air-tight freezer container or resealable plastic freezer bag. Remove muffins one at a time and warm in microwave oven, if desired. If you wish to freeze *Carrot-Raisin Oat Muffins*, prepare without cream cheese topping.

The **Lemon/Zester Scorer** is the perfect tool for zesting any citrus fruit. It works best for this recipe if you zest with short strokes.

Spiced Pumpkin Mini Loaves

This delicately spiced tea bread would make a fine accompaniment to any brunch or teatime spread.

PREP TIME: 25 MINUTES   BAKE TIME: 45-50 MINUTES   COOL TIME: 1 HOUR

Bread

2 1/4	**cups all-purpose flour**
1	**cup sugar**
1	**cup golden raisins**
1/2	**cup pecan halves, coarsely chopped**
1	**tablespoon** *Pantry Cinnamon Plus Spice Blend*
2	**teaspoons baking powder**
1/2	**teaspoon baking soda**
1/2	**teaspoon salt**
2	**eggs**
1	**cup solid pack pumpkin**
2/3	**cup milk**
1/2	**cup vegetable oil**

Glaze

1/2	**cup powdered sugar**
1/4	**teaspoon** *Pantry Cinnamon Plus Spice Blend*
2-3	**tablespoons maple-flavored syrup**
	Additional toasted chopped pecans (optional)

1. Preheat oven to 325°F. Spray bottoms only of **Mini Loaf Pan** with nonstick cooking spray. In **Stainless (2-qt.) Mixing Bowl**, combine flour, sugar, raisins, pecans, spice blend, baking powder, baking soda and salt; mix well.

2. In **Stainless (4-qt.) Mixing Bowl**, whisk eggs with **Stainless Whisk**. Add pumpkin, milk and oil; mix well. Add flour mixture to egg mixture; mix until well blended. Fill each cavity of loaf pan with about 1 cup batter.

3. Bake 45-50 minutes or until **Cake Tester** inserted in centers of loaves comes out clean and cracks in tops of loaves appear dry. Remove from oven; cool in pan 10 minutes. Loosen sides of loaves from pan; remove to **Stackable Cooling Rack**. Cool completely.

4. For glaze, combine powdered sugar and spice blend. Whisk in 2-3 tablespoons maple-flavored syrup until icing is of desired consistency. Drizzle icing over loaves and sprinkle with additional toasted chopped pecans, if desired.

Yield: 16 servings

Nutrients per serving (2 slices): Calories 260, Total Fat 10 g, Saturated Fat 1 g, Cholesterol 25 mg, Carbohydrate 41 g, Protein 4 g, Sodium 190 mg, Fiber 2 g

Diabetic exchanges per serving: 1 starch, 1 1/2 fruit, 2 fat (2 1/2 carb)

Pumpkin pie spice can be substituted for the Cinnamon Plus Spice Blend, if desired.

Be sure to choose solid pack pumpkin, rather than pumpkin pie filling, for this recipe.

To make loaves well in advance, prepare as directed in Steps 1-3. Wrap securely; freeze up to 1 month. When ready to serve, thaw bread at room temperature and unwrap. Prepare glaze and drizzle over bread.

This recipe can be baked in the **Stoneware Loaf Pan**. Spray bottom only of loaf pan with nonstick cooking spray. Prepare as recipe directs; pour batter into pan. Bake at 325°F 1 hour, 10 minutes to 1 hour, 20 minutes or until Cake Tester inserted in center comes out clean.

Blueberry-Almond Oat Muffins (p. 73), *Carrot-Raisin Oat Muffins* (p. 73), *Dutch Apple Oat Muffins* (p. 73), *Spiced Pumpkin Mini Loaves*

Mexican Chocolate Cream Pie

Accented with our Korintje Cinnamon, this rich and creamy pie is a fabulous casual dessert.

PREP TIME: 30 MINUTES   BAKE TIME: 10-12 MINUTES   CHILL TIME: 30 MINUTES

1   refrigerated pie crust (from 15-ounce package), softened as directed on package

1/2   cup semi-sweet chocolate morsels, divided

1   container (12 ounces) frozen whipped topping, thawed, divided

1   package (8 ounces) cream cheese, softened

1   cup milk

1   package (3.9 ounces) chocolate instant pudding and pie filling

1   teaspoon *Pantry Korintje Cinnamon*

1. Preheat oven to 425°F. Gently unroll crust onto lightly floured surface. Roll to an 11½-inch circle using lightly floured **Baker's Roller**™. Place crust in **Deep Dish Pie Plate**, pressing dough into bottom and up sides. Prick bottom and sides using pastry tool. Bake 10-12 minutes or until light golden brown. Remove from oven; cool completely.

2. Reserve 1 tablespoon of the chocolate morsels for garnish. Place remaining chocolate morsels in **Small Micro-Cooker**®. Microwave, uncovered, on HIGH 1 minute, stirring every 10 seconds, until melted and smooth. Do not overheat. Using **Skinny Scraper**, spread chocolate over bottom and 1 inch up sides of pie crust.

3. Attach open star tip to **Easy Accent**® **Decorator** and fill with 1 cup of the whipped topping; set aside. Whisk cream cheese in **Classic Batter Bowl** with **Stainless Whisk** until smooth. Gradually whisk in milk until well blended. Add pudding mix all at once and cinnamon; whisk until smooth (mixture will be very thick). Fold in remaining whipped topping. Spoon filling into crust, spreading evenly using **Small Spreader**.

4. Using **Deluxe Cheese Grater**, grate reserved chocolate morsels over top of pie. Pipe a decorative border of whipped topping around edge of pie; sprinkle with additional cinnamon, if desired. Refrigerate at least 30 minutes or until ready to serve. Cut into wedges using **Utility Knife**.

Yield: 12 servings

Nutrients per serving: Calories 460, Total Fat 28 g, Saturated Fat 18 g, Cholesterol 35 mg, Carbohydrate 44 g, Protein 4 g, Sodium 400 mg, Fiber less than 1 g

Diabetic exchanges per serving: 1 starch, 1 fruit, 3½ fat (2 carb)

Ground cinnamon can be substituted for the Korintje Cinnamon, if desired.

To soften cream cheese, microwave on HIGH 15-30 seconds or until softened.

Because the chocolate layer on the pie crust hardens during refrigeration, press down firmly with the Utility Knife when cutting the pie into wedges.

Croissant Bread Pudding

Sweet comfort! This warm, rich dessert is topped with a rum-flavored sauce that is simply divine.

PREP TIME: 15 MINUTES   BAKE TIME: 30-35 MINUTES

4 **large croissants (about 3 ounces each)**

1 **red baking apple such as Jonathan**

6 **eggs**

1/2 **cup plus 3 tablespoons sugar, divided**

2 **cups half and half**

1 **orange**

1/2 **cup pecan halves, chopped**

3/4 **cup butterscotch caramel ice cream topping**

1/4 **teaspoon rum extract**

1/2 **cup golden raisins**

1. Preheat oven to 350°F. Lightly spray **Deep Dish Baker** with nonstick cooking spray. Slice croissants from top to bottom into 1/2-inch slices. Set aside 16 of the largest slices. Cube remaining slices and place in bottom of baker. Arrange reserved slices over cubes in an overlapping circular pattern. Using **Apple Peeler/Corer/Slicer**, core and slice apple, leaving peel on; cut slices in half. Tuck apple slices between croissant slices.

2. In **Classic Batter Bowl**, whisk eggs and 1/2 cup of the sugar. Pour half and half into **Large Micro-Cooker®**; microwave on HIGH 2 minutes or until hot. Slowly add half and half to egg mixture; whisk using **Stainless Whisk** until well blended. Carefully pour egg mixture over croissants. If necessary, lightly press croissants down to coat.

3. Zest orange using **Lemon Zester/Scorer** to measure 2 teaspoons zest. Using **Juicer**, juice orange to measure 1/4 cup juice; set juice aside. Chop pecans using **Food Chopper**. Combine remaining sugar, orange zest and pecans; sprinkle over croissants. Bake 30-35 minutes or until golden brown and set in center. Remove from oven to **Stackable Cooling Rack**; let stand 10 minutes.

4. Meanwhile, combine ice cream topping, rum extract, reserved orange juice and raisins in **Small Micro-Cooker®**. Microwave on HIGH 30-60 seconds or until hot; pour into serving bowl. Serve sauce over pudding.

Yield: 12 servings

Nutrients per serving: Calories 280, Total Fat 12 g, Saturated Fat 6 g, Cholesterol 110 mg, Carbohydrate 36 g, Protein 6 g, Sodium 230 mg, Fiber 1 g

Diabetic exchanges per serving: 2 starch, 1/2 fruit, 2 fat (2 1/2 carb)

cook's tips

This recipe can be prepared in the **Oval Baker**, if desired. Preheat oven to 325°F. Prepare as recipe directs; bake 45-50 minutes.

Large croissants can be found in the bakery section of most grocery stores.

Sweetened dried cranberries or regular raisins can be substituted for the golden raisins, if desired.

For cooking and baking, use apples that are flavorful and that are firm enough to hold up to cooking, such as Jonathan, Rome Beauty or Cortland.

Mocha Cappuccino Cake

It's easy to achieve professional-looking results on this beautifully garnished cake with the Easy Accent® Decorator and Deluxe Cheese Grater.

PREP TIME: 30 MINUTES   BAKE TIME: 40-45 MINUTES   COOL TIME: 1 HOUR

1 package (18.25 ounces) devil's food cake mix (plus ingredients to make cake)

1/4 cup granulated sugar

2 tablespoons instant coffee granules, divided

1/3 cup boiling water

1 package (8 ounces) cream cheese, softened

1 cup powdered sugar

1 container (8 ounces) frozen whipped topping, thawed

1/4 cup semi-sweet chocolate morsels, grated

1. Preheat oven to 350°F. Spray bottom only of **Deep Dish Baker** with nonstick cooking spray. Prepare cake mix according to package directions; pour batter into baker. Bake 40-45 minutes or until **Cake Tester** inserted in center comes out clean. Cool on **Stackable Cooling Rack** 15 minutes. Remove from baker; cool completely.

2. In **Small Batter Bowl**, combine granulated sugar, 1/2 tablespoon of the instant coffee granules and boiling water; stir until dissolved and set aside. In **Classic Batter Bowl**, combine cream cheese, powdered sugar and remaining 1 1/2 tablespoons coffee granules; whisk until smooth using **Stainless Whisk**. Fold whipped topping into cream cheese mixture using **Classic Scraper**. Place 1 cup of the cream cheese filling into **Easy Accent®Decorator**; set aside for garnish.

3. Using **Serrated Bread Knife**, cut cake in half horizontally to form two even layers. Carefully remove top layer using **Lift & Serve™**; set aside. Brush half of the coffee mixture over bottom cake layer using **Pastry Brush**. Spread remaining cream cheese filling over cake layer using **Large Spreader**. Grate half of the chocolate morsels over filling using **Deluxe Cheese Grater** fitted with coarse grating drum. Carefully top with second cake layer. Brush top and sides of cake with remaining coffee mixture. Pipe rosettes of filling around edge of cake using decorator. Grate remaining chocolate over cake.

Yield: 16 servings

Nutrients per serving: Calories 360, Total Fat 19 g, Saturated Fat 8 g, Cholesterol 55 mg, Carbohydrate 42 g, Protein 4 g, Sodium 340 mg, Fiber less than 1 g

Diabetic exchanges per serving: 1 starch, 2 fruit, 3 1/2 fat (3 carb)

cook's tips

To easily cut cakes into layers, mark the middle points on the sides of the cake with several wooden picks. Using the picks as a guide, cut through the center of the cake using Serrated Bread Knife.

To soften cream cheese, microwave on HIGH 15-30 seconds or until softened.

If desired, 1 bar (1.55 ounces) milk chocolate can be substituted for the chocolate morsels.

Double Berry Galette

A galette is a rustic, free-form tart, usually filled with fruit. The result is a juicy pastry that begs for a sprinkle of powdered sugar or ice cream.

PREP TIME: 15 MINUTES   BAKE TIME: 35-37 MINUTES   COOL TIME: 30 MINUTES

1   lemon
3   cups blueberries, divided
1   cup raspberries, divided
1/4   cup granulated sugar
1   tablespoon all-purpose flour
1/8   teaspoon *Pantry Korintje Cinnamon*
1   refrigerated pie crust (from
      15-ounce package), softened
      as directed on package
      Powdered sugar

1. Preheat oven to 375°F. Zest lemon using **Microplane® Adjustable Grater** to measure 1 tablespoon zest; set aside. Juice lemon using **Juicer** to measure 2 teaspoons juice. Combine lemon juice, 1 cup of the blueberries, 1/2 cup of the raspberries, granulated sugar, flour and cinnamon in **Small Batter Bowl**; toss gently to coat using **Small Mix 'N Scraper®**.

2. Gently unroll pie crust onto center of **Small Round Stone**. Spoon berry mixture evenly over crust to within 1 1/2 inches of edge of crust. Fold outer edge of crust up over filling, overlapping every 2 inches to form an even border.

3. Bake 35-37 minutes or until filling is bubbly in center and crust is golden brown. Remove from oven to **Stackable Cooling Rack**. Sprinkle with remaining berries; cool 30 minutes. Sprinkle with powdered sugar using **Flour/Sugar Shaker**. Garnish with reserved lemon zest. Cut into wedges using **Slice 'N Serve**™.

Yield: 8 servings

Nutrients per serving: Calories 180, Total Fat 7 g, Saturated Fat 3 g, Cholesterol 5 mg, Carbohydrate 29 g, Protein 2 g, Sodium 100 mg, Fiber 2 g

Diabetic exchanges per serving: 1 starch, 1 fruit, 1 fat (2 carb)

cook's tips

Ground cinnamon can be substituted for the Korintje Cinnamon, if desired.

Place a sheet of aluminum foil on the oven rack below the baking stone to catch any drippings.

To quickly bring pie crust to room temperature, place the crust pouch in the microwave; microwave on DEFROST (30% power) for 10-20 seconds.

To keep berries fresh, do not wash them until you're ready to use them. Arrange them in a single layer on a paper towel-lined plate. Cover with additional paper towels and refrigerate up to 2 days before using.

Cherry-Chocolate Coffee Cake

Convenient coffee cake mix and cherry pie filling help you to prepare a delicious brunch treat in just 10 minutes.

PREP TIME: 10 MINUTES   BAKE TIME: 41-43 MINUTES   COOL TIME: 1 HOUR

- **1**   **package (26.5 ounces) cinnamon streusel coffee cake mix**
- **1 1/4**   **cups water**
- **1/3**   **cup vegetable oil**
- **3**   **eggs**
- **1**   **cup semi-sweet chocolate morsels, divided**
- **1**   **can (21 ounce) cherry pie filling**
- **1/2**   **cup pecan halves, coarsely chopped**

1. Preheat oven to 350°F. Spray bottom only of **Rectangular Baker** with nonstick cooking spray. Set aside streusel topping and glaze packets. Combine cake mix, water, oil and eggs in **Stainless (4-qt.) Mixing Bowl**; mix according to package directions. Gently stir in 1/2 cup of the chocolate morsels with **Small Mix 'N Scraper®**. Spread batter evenly in baker.

2. Drain cherry pie filling in small **Colander**, shaking out excess glaze. (Do not rinse cherries.) Spoon cherries evenly over batter. Coarsely chop pecans using **Food Chopper**. Combine pecans, remaining 1/2 cup chocolate morsels and streusel topping in **Small Batter Bowl**; sprinkle over cherries.

3. Bake 41-43 minutes or until **Cake Tester** inserted in center comes out clean. Remove from oven to **Stackable Cooling Rack**; cool 1 hour.

4. Prepare glaze packet according to package directions. Drizzle glaze over slightly warm cake. Cut cake into squares; serve using **Mini-Serving Spatula**.

Yield: 15 servings

Nutrients per serving: Calories 380, Total Fat 17 g, Saturated Fat 4 g, Cholesterol 40 mg, Carbohydrate 56 g, Protein 3 g, Sodium 260 mg, Fiber 0 g

Diabetic exchanges per serving: 1 starch, 3 fruit, 3 fat (4 carb)

Removing excess glaze from the cherry pie filling helps prevent the cherries from forming deep pockets in the finished coffee cake.

To make cutting and serving this tender coffee cake easier, it needs to be almost completely cool.

Truffle Brownies

Simply decadent, these frosted brownies will hit the spot when your family craves something sweet.

PREP TIME: 15 MINUTES   BAKE TIME: 25-28 MINUTES   COOL TIME: 1 HOUR

Brownies

- 1½ cups all-purpose flour
- ½ teaspoon baking soda
- ½ teaspoon salt
- ¾ cup butter or margarine
- 4 squares (4 ounces) unsweetened baking chocolate
- 1½ cups packed brown sugar
- 3 eggs
- 2 tablespoons water
- ½ teaspoon *Pantry Double Strength Vanilla*

Frosting

- 1 square (1 ounce) unsweetened baking chocolate
- 2 tablespoons butter or margarine
- 1 cup thawed, frozen whipped topping
- 1¼ cups powdered sugar

1. Preheat oven to 325°F. Spray bottom only of **Medium Bar Pan** with nonstick cooking spray. For brownies, in **Small Batter Bowl**, combine flour, baking soda and salt; mix well.

2. Place butter and chocolate in **Classic Batter Bowl**. Microwave, uncovered, on HIGH 1 minute; stir. Microwave an additional 15-30 seconds or until chocolate is completely melted, stirring after 15 seconds. Stir brown sugar into chocolate mixture until well blended. Add eggs, water and vanilla; mix well. Add flour mixture; mix until well blended.

3. Pour batter into pan. Bake 25-28 minutes or until **Cake Tester** inserted in center comes out almost clean. Do not overbake. Remove from oven to **Stackable Cooling Rack**; cool completely.

4. For frosting, place chocolate and butter in **Small Micro-Cooker®**. Microwave, uncovered, on HIGH 1 minute-1 minute, 15 seconds or until chocolate is melted and smooth, stirring after each 15-second interval. Add whipped topping; microwave on HIGH 15 seconds and stir until completely blended. Add powdered sugar; mix until smooth. Immediately spread frosting evenly over cooled brownie using **Small Spreader**. Let stand until frosting is set; cut into bars.

Yield: 24 bars

Nutrients per serving (1 bar): Calories 440, Total Fat 11 g, Saturated Fat 7 g, Cholesterol 45 mg, Carbohydrate 86 g, Protein 4 g, Sodium 150 mg, Fiber 2 g

Diabetic exchanges per serving (1 bar): 1 starch, 4½ fruit, 2 fat (5½ carb)

Create-a-Cookie (p. 88),
Pecan Praline Cookie Triangles (p. 89),
Truffle Brownies

cook's tips

If desired, 1 teaspoon vanilla can be substituted for the Double Strength Vanilla.

The frosting sets up very quickly. Be sure to spread it quickly to ensure a smooth surface.

Stoneware absorbs and distributes heat evenly. The result is a pan of brownies that are fudgy and decadent all the way through. No more overbaked edges!

Chocolate can scorch easily, even in the microwave. Be sure to stir it often, and do not overheat it.

Create-a-Cookie

Here's an easy way to get three different varieties of cookies from one batch of dough. Choose your three favorite toppings for a personalized combination!

PREP TIME: 10 MINUTES   BAKE TIME: 10-16 MINUTES PER BATCH

If desired, 1 teaspoon vanilla can be substituted for the Double Strength Vanilla.

The first batch of cookies baked on a baking stone may require 1-2 more minutes of bake time. After the first batch, the time range indicated in the recipe should yield good results.

Cool cookies for 2-3 minutes before transferring them from the baking stone to the Stackable Cooling Rack. This will prevent broken or "wrinkled" cookies.

If you have only one baking stone, portion the cookie dough onto **Parchment Paper**, cut to the diameter of the baking stone. As you remove one batch of cookies from the oven, place another parchment sheet of dough on the baking stone and into the oven.

3	**cups all-purpose flour**	
1	**teaspoon baking soda**	
1/2	**teaspoon salt**	
1	**cup (2 sticks) butter or margarine, softened**	
1 1/2	**cups packed brown sugar**	
1/2	**cup granulated sugar**	
2	**eggs**	
1/2	**teaspoon** *Pantry Double Strength Vanilla*	
3	*Toppings* **(see below)**	

1. Preheat oven to 375°F. Combine flour, baking soda and salt in **Classic Batter Bowl**; mix well. In **Stainless (4-qt.) Mixing Bowl**, beat butter, brown sugar and granulated sugar until creamy. Add eggs and vanilla; beat well. Gradually beat in flour mixture.

2. Choose three *Toppings*; place into separate **Prep Bowls**. Using **Medium Scoop**, drop level scoops of dough 2 inches apart onto **Rectangle Stone**. (Cookies will spread during baking.) Flatten scoops slightly with palm of hand. Lightly press toppings into tops of cookies.

3. Bake 10-16 minutes or until cookies are almost set. (Centers will be soft. Do not overbake.) Remove from oven; cool 2 minutes on baking stone. Using **Mini-Serving Spatula**, remove cookies to **Stackable Cooling Rack**. Cool completely. Repeat with remaining dough.

Yield: About 3 dozen cookies

Nutrients per serving (1 cookie plus combined average of toppings): Calories 240, Total Fat 6 g, Saturated Fat 3.5 g, Cholesterol 25 mg, Carbohydrate 45 g, Protein 2 g, Sodium 125 mg, Fiber 0 g

Diabetic exchanges per serving (1 cookie plus combined average of toppings): 1 starch, 2 fruit, 1 fat (3 carb)

	Chocolate Candy Bars	Chocolate-Coated Candies	Chocolate Peanut Butter Cups	Chopped Nuts	Cinnamon 'N Sugar
Toppings	2 bars (about 1.5 ounces each) chocolate candy	1/4 cup chocolate-coated candy pieces	12 mini chocolate peanut butter cups, cut into quarters	1/3 cup coarsely chopped nuts	1 tablespoon sugar combined with 1/8 teaspoon ground cinnamon

Pecan Praline Cookie Triangles

As sweet as pecan pie but with a sinfully tender, buttery crust, these cookies will be sure to disappear at your next get-together.

PREP TIME: 15 MINUTES   BAKE TIME: 32-34 MINUTES   COOL TIME: 2 HOURS

Crust

2½	cups all-purpose flour
¾	cup powdered sugar
1	teaspoon baking soda
¾	cup (1½ sticks) butter or margarine, melted

Filling

3	cups pecan halves, divided
2	cups packed brown sugar
3	eggs
4	tablespoons butter or margarine, melted
1	teaspoon *Pantry Double Strength Vanilla*
¼	teaspoon salt
	Powdered sugar (optional)

1. Preheat oven to 350°F. For crust, combine flour, powdered sugar and baking soda in **Classic Batter Bowl**. Add butter; mix until crumbly using **Classic Scraper**. Lightly press crumb mixture over bottom of **Stoneware Bar Pan**; roll lightly using **Baker's Roller™**. Bake 15 minutes; remove from oven to **Stackable Cooling Rack**.

2. Meanwhile, for filling, reserve 1 cup of the pecans for garnish; chop remaining pecans using **Food Chopper**. Combine chopped pecans, brown sugar, eggs, butter, vanilla and salt; mix well. Pour filling over warm crust, spreading to edges of pan using **Large Spreader**. Arrange remaining pecan halves over filling. Bake 17-19 minutes or until filling is set in center. Remove from oven; cool completely.

3. Sprinkle with additional powdered sugar, if desired. Cut into 32 squares using **Utility Knife**; cut each square in half diagonally.

Yield: 64 triangles

Nutrients per serving (1 triangle): Calories 110, Total Fat 7 g, Saturated Fat 2 g, Cholesterol 15 mg, Carbohydrate 12 g, Protein 1 g, Sodium 55 mg, Fiber less than 1 g

Diabetic exchanges per serving (1 triangle): 1 fruit, 1 fat (1 carb)

If desired, 2 teaspoons vanilla can be substituted for the Double Strength Vanilla.

To store leftover cookies, place in tightly covered container at room temperature.

Butter lends a rich flavor and tender crust and is preferred over margarine in this recipe.

For easier serving, line Stoneware Bar Pan with a 13-inch piece of **Parchment Paper**. Prepare recipe as directed and cool completely, then simply lift Parchment Paper out of pan and cut as directed.

Upside-Down Caramel Apple Pie

*Serve this candied apple pie upside-down to reveal the
rich caramel-pecan topping.*

PREP TIME: 30 MINUTES   BAKE TIME: 55-60 MINUTES   COOL TIME: 1 HOUR

Glaze and Pastry

- 1/4 **cup packed brown sugar**
- 1 **tablespoon butter or margarine, melted**
- 1 **tablespoon light corn syrup**
- 1/3 **cup pecan halves, coarsely chopped**
- 1 **package (15 ounces) refrigerated pie crusts, softened as directed on package**

Filling

- 6 **large Granny Smith apples (about 6 cups slices)**
- 1 **tablespoon lemon juice**
- 3/4 **cup packed brown sugar**
- 1/3 **cup all-purpose flour**
- 1 **teaspoon** *Pantry Korintje Cinnamon*
- 1 **teaspoon lemon zest**

1. Preheat oven to 425°F. For glaze, combine brown sugar, butter and corn syrup in **Deep Dish Pie Plate**; spread evenly over bottom. Chop pecans using **Food Chopper**; sprinkle over sugar mixture. Gently unroll one pie crust; place in pie plate, pressing into bottom and up sides. Set aside.

2. For filling, peel, core and slice apples using **Apple Peeler/Corer/Slicer**; cut slices in half. In **Stainless (4-qt.) Mixing Bowl**, combine apples and lemon juice; toss gently to coat. Add brown sugar, flour, cinnamon and lemon zest; mix gently. Spoon filling into pie plate. Unroll remaining crust and place over filling. Fold edges of top crust under edges of bottom crust; seal and flute edges. Cut slits in top crust to allow steam to escape.

3. Gently place **Pie Crust Shield** or 2- to 3-inch-wide strips of aluminum foil over edge of pie. Bake 30 minutes; remove shield. Bake an additional 25-30 minutes or until crust is deep golden brown. Remove from oven to **Stackable Cooling Rack**; let stand 5 minutes. Loosen edge of pie from pie plate; carefully invert pie onto heat-resistant serving plate. Scrape any remaining caramel topping from pie plate onto top of pie. Cool at least 1 hour before serving.

Yield: 8 servings

Nutrients per serving: Calories 460, Total Fat 19 g, Saturated Fat 7 g, Cholesterol 15 mg, Carbohydrate 72 g, Protein 3 g, Sodium 220 mg, Fiber 3 g

Diabetic exchanges per serving: 1 starch, 3 1/2 fruit, 3 1/2 fat (4 1/2 carb)

Ground cinnamon can be substituted for the Korintje Cinnamon, if desired.

Place a sheet of aluminum foil on the oven rack below the pie plate to catch any drippings.

This recipe is based on *tarte Tatin*, an inverted caramel apple pie that was created and sold by the Tatin sisters in France.

Granny Smith apples are wonderful for pies because of their firm texture and sweet-tart flavor that hold up during baking.

The **Mix 'N Scraper®** is the perfect tool to rescue any caramel that sticks to the bottom of the Deep Dish Pie Plate. It is heat-resistant, so it won't melt while in contact with Stoneware.

Lemon Poppy Seed Pound Cake

This classic pound cake is tender with a heavenly lemon flavor.

PREP TIME: 10 MINUTES   BAKE TIME: 55-60 MINUTES   COOL TIME: 1 HOUR, 30 MINUTES

1½ cups all-purpose flour
1½ cups granulated sugar
2 tablespoons lemon zest
2 tablespoons poppy seeds
1 teaspoon baking powder
½ teaspoon salt
¾ cup (1½ sticks) butter, softened (do not substitute margarine)
4 ounces cream cheese, softened
4 eggs
2 tablespoons milk
1 teaspoon *Pantry Double Strength Vanilla*
Powdered sugar (optional)

1. Preheat oven to 325°F. Spray **Stoneware Fluted Pan** with nonstick cooking spray. Combine flour, granulated sugar, lemon zest, poppy seeds, baking powder and salt in **Stainless (2-qt.) Mixing Bowl**; mix well. In **Stainless (4-qt.) Mixing Bowl**, beat butter and cream cheese on high speed of hand-held electric mixer 1 minute. Add flour mixture; beat on low speed 1 minute or until blended (mixture will form a stiff paste).

2. In **Small Batter Bowl**, whisk eggs, milk and vanilla just until blended. Add egg mixture to cream cheese mixture in four additions, beating 2 minutes after each addition. (Do not undermix.)

3. Pour batter into pan. Bake 55-60 minutes or until **Cake Tester** inserted near center comes out clean. Cool cake in pan 10 minutes. Loosen cake from sides of pan; carefully invert onto **Stackable Cooling Rack**, keeping pan over cake. Cool completely.

4. Place cake on serving platter. Sprinkle with powdered sugar or prepare glaze, if desired (see Cook's Tip).

Yield: 16 servings

Nutrients per serving: Calories 430, Total Fat 12 g, Saturated Fat 7 g, Cholesterol 85 mg, Carbohydrate 78 g, Protein 3 g, Sodium 200 mg, Fiber 0 g

Diabetic exchanges per serving: 1 starch, 4 fruit, 2½ fat (5 carb)

Variation: *Sweetheart Mini Pound Cakes:*
Spray **Mini Fluted Pan** with nonstick cooking spray. Prepare as recipe directs through Step 2. Spoon batter evenly into wells of pan (about ¾ cup batter per well); bake 30-35 minutes or until Cake Tester inserted near centers of cakes comes out clean. Cool as recipe directs. Sprinkle with powdered sugar or prepare glaze, if desired (see Cook's Tip).

Yield: 6 mini pound cakes (12 servings)

For glaze, combine 1½ cups powdered sugar and enough lemon juice to make a thick frosting (4-5 teaspoons). Spread glaze over top of cake.

To make and glaze this cake, you will need two lemons. The **Microplane® Adjustable Grater** grates zest finely for a balanced lemon flavor in every bite.

If desired, 2 teaspoons vanilla can be substituted for the Double Strength Vanilla.

For best results, it is important to bring the butter, cream cheese and eggs to room temperature before mixing.

Make sure to beat the batter for the length of time the recipe directs. Undermixing the batter will result in low volume and dense cakes.

table for
two

Choose from this classy menu
of appetizers, main dishes and
desserts and light the candles. It
will be just the two of you tonight.

Baked Pesto Salmon (p. 96)

cook's tips

30

minutes or less

Pantry Basil Oil can be substituted for the olive oil, if desired.

To test fish for doneness, flake it with a fork at its thickest point. It should flake easily and be opaque throughout.

Prepared basil pesto is a flavorful sauce made with basil, garlic, pine nuts, Parmesan cheese and olive oil. It can be found near the refrigerated fresh pasta in the supermarket.

The ingredients in this recipe can be easily doubled and baked on the **Stoneware Bar Pan**.

Baked Pesto Salmon

Salmon fillets reach whole new heights of flavor when a pesto and lemon juice sauce is brushed over them before baking. Colorful vegetables round out the meal.

PREP TIME: 10 MINUTES   BAKE TIME: 12-14 MINUTES

2   **salmon fillets (4-6 ounces each), about 1 inch thick**

2   **small yellow summer squash or zucchini, cut into 1-inch slices**

1   **small red onion, cut into 1-inch wedges**

1   **tablespoon olive oil**

1   **garlic clove, pressed**

1/4   **teaspoon salt**

1/8   **teaspoon ground black pepper**

1   **lemon**

2   **tablespoons prepared basil pesto**

1. Preheat oven to 425°F. Place salmon fillets side by side but not touching on **Medium Bar Pan**.

2. Cut yellow squash crosswise into 1-inch slices using **Crinkle Cutter**; cut slices in half. Cut onion into 1-inch wedges using **Utility Knife**. In **Small Batter Bowl**, combine oil, garlic pressed with **Garlic Press**, salt and black pepper. Add vegetables; toss to coat. Arrange vegetables around salmon on pan.

3. Zest lemon using **Lemon Zester/Scorer** to measure 1/2 teaspoon zest. Juice lemon using **Juicer** to measure 2 teaspoons juice. In **Prep Bowl**, combine lemon zest, juice and pesto; mix well. Brush top and sides of salmon with pesto mixture using **Pastry Brush**. Bake 12-14 minutes or until salmon flakes easily with fork and vegetables are crisp-tender. Garnish with additional lemon zest, if desired.

Yield: 2 servings

Nutrients per serving: Calories 370, Total Fat 25 g, Saturated Fat 5 g, Cholesterol 70 mg, Carbohydrate 10 g, Protein 26 g, Sodium 490 mg, Fiber 3 g

Diabetic exchanges per serving: 1 starch, 3 high-fat meat (2 carb)

Shrimp-Stuffed Portobello Mushrooms

A creamy filling studded with chopped shrimp elevates regular stuffed mushrooms to delicious new heights. (Pictured on the cover.)

PREP TIME: 15 MINUTES   BAKE TIME: 18-20 MINUTES

cook's tips

Mushrooms and Shrimp Filling

- **2   medium portobello mushroom caps (3-4 inches in diameter)**
- **3   ounces shelled, deveined, cooked shrimp, chopped**
- **2   tablespoons (1/2 ounce) grated fresh Parmesan cheese**
- **1   lemon**
- **1   teaspoon snipped fresh parsley**
- **3   tablespoons chive and onion cream cheese spread**
- **1/4   teaspoon Dijon mustard**
- **1/2   small garlic clove, pressed**

Crumb Topping

- **2   teaspoons butter or margarine**
- **1/2   small garlic clove, pressed**
- **1 1/2   tablespoons unseasoned dry bread crumbs**

1. Preheat oven to 400°F. For mushrooms, place mushrooms, gill sides up, on **Small Bar Pan**.

2. For shrimp filling, chop shrimp using **Food Chopper**. Grate Parmesan cheese using **Deluxe Cheese Grater**. Zest lemon using **Microplane® Adjustable Grater** to measure 2 teaspoons zest. Snip parsley using **Kitchen Shears**. In **Classic Batter Bowl**, combine shrimp, Parmesan cheese, lemon zest, parsley, cream cheese spread, mustard and garlic pressed with **Garlic Press**; mix well. Divide shrimp mixture into two equal portions; spoon into mushroom caps and flatten slightly.

3. For crumb topping, place butter and garlic pressed with Garlic Press in **Prep Bowl**; microwave on HIGH 20-30 seconds or until butter is melted. Stir in bread crumbs. Sprinkle crumb topping evenly over shrimp filling. Bake 18-20 minutes or until crumb topping is golden brown and filling is hot. Serve warm.

Yield: 2 servings

Nutrients per serving (1 stuffed mushroom): Calories 200, Total Fat 13 g, Saturated Fat 7 g, Cholesterol 35 mg, Carbohydrate 10 g, Protein 13 g, Sodium 270 mg, Fiber 2 g

Diabetic exchanges per serving (1 stuffed mushroom): 1/2 starch, 2 medium-fat meat (1/2 carb)

To remove dirt from mushrooms, wipe mushrooms with a damp paper towel or soft brush, or quickly rinse them under cold running water and immediately pat dry. Do not clean mushrooms until you're ready to use them.

Imitation crabmeat can be substituted for the shrimp, if desired.

If desired, six large button mushrooms can be substituted for the portobello mushrooms. Remove stems; discard or reserve for another use. Proceed as recipe directs.

This recipe can be easily doubled and baked on the **Medium Bar Pan**.

Greek Pita Pizzas

*Cool, fresh vegetables top warm, crispy pita crusts
for a refreshing lunch or hearty snack.*

PREP TIME: 15 MINUTES   BAKE TIME: 7-9 MINUTES

- ¼ **cup pitted kalamata olives, coarsely chopped**
- 2 **flat pita bread rounds (without pockets)**
- ¼ **cup crumbled feta cheese**
- 1 **large plum tomato, seeded and diced**
- ¼ **cup peeled, seeded and chopped cucumber**
- 2 **tablespoons chopped red onion**
- 1 **tablespoon snipped fresh mint leaves**
- 2 **teaspoons olive oil**
  Plain yogurt or sour cream (optional)

1. Preheat oven to 450°F. Coarsely chop olives using **Food Chopper**. Place pita rounds on **Rectangle Stone**. Sprinkle with olives and feta cheese. Bake 7-9 minutes or until cheese is lightly browned.

2. Meanwhile, slice tomato in half crosswise using **Chef's Knife**; remove seeds using **Cook's Corer™** and dice. Chop cucumber and onion using Food Chopper. Combine tomato, cucumber, onion, mint and oil in **Small Batter Bowl**; mix using **Small Mix 'N Scraper®**.

3. Top pita rounds evenly with tomato mixture. Drizzle with yogurt, if desired, and serve immediately.

Yield: 2 servings

Nutrients per serving: Calories 320, Total Fat 15 g, Saturated Fat 4 g, Cholesterol 15 mg, Carbohydrate 37 g, Protein 9 g, Sodium 510 mg, Fiber 4 g

Diabetic exchanges per serving: 2 starch, 1 vegetable, 3 fat (2 carb)

cook's tips

minutes or less

This recipe can be easily doubled and baked on the **Rectangle Stone**.

Pantry Basil Oil can be substituted for the olive oil, if desired.

Kalamata olives can be found in the deli section or in jars in the condiment section of most supermarkets. Pitted, ripe olives can be substituted for the kalamata olives, if desired.

If you cannot find pitted kalamata olives, never fear. The **Cherry/Olive Pitter** makes quick work of pitting olives. Place one olive, pointed end down, into the pitter and squeeze the arms over a bowl to catch the falling pit.

Easy Nachos for Two

The combination of corn kernels and queso fresco, as well as blue corn chips, creates a special appetizer for just the two of you.

PREP TIME: 15 MINUTES   BAKE TIME: 6-9 MINUTES

Salsa

1	large plum tomato, seeded and diced
1	large jalapeño pepper, seeded and finely chopped
1/4	cup frozen whole kernel corn, thawed
2	tablespoons thick and chunky salsa
1	tablespoon snipped fresh cilantro
1/4	teaspoon salt

Nachos

30	blue corn tortilla chips (about 1 1/2 cups chips)
1/4	cup (1 ounce) crumbled queso fresco
1/2	cup (2 ounces) shredded Mexican cheese blend, divided
	Lime wedges (optional)

1. Preheat oven to 425°F. For salsa, slice tomato in half crosswise using **Chef's Knife**; remove seeds using **Cook's Corer**™ and dice. Finely chop jalapeño pepper using **Food Chopper**. In **Small Batter Bowl**, combine tomato, jalapeño pepper, corn, salsa, cilantro and salt; mix well.

2. For nachos, arrange tortilla chips on **Small Round Stone**. Top chips with queso fresco, half of the Mexican cheese blend and salsa.

3. Bake 5-7 minutes or until cheese begins to melt. Sprinkle with remaining 1/4 cup Mexican cheese blend; bake 1-2 minutes or until cheese begins to melt. Remove from oven; squeeze lime wedges over nachos, if desired. Serve immediately.

Yield: 2 servings

Nutrients per serving: Calories 280, Total Fat 16 g, Saturated Fat 7 g, Cholesterol 25 mg, Carbohydrate 27 g, Protein 10 g, Sodium 680 mg, Fiber 4 g

Diabetic exchanges per serving: 1 1/2 starch, 1 high-fat meat, 1 1/2 fat (1 1/2 carb)

cook's tips

30

minutes or less

This recipe can be easily doubled and baked on the **Large Round Stone**.

Blue corn chips are often found in the organic sections of most grocery stores. Yellow or white corn chips can be substituted for the blue corn chips, if desired.

Queso fresco is a fresh, white Mexican cheese that is traditionally crumbled over foods and used to fill enchiladas. It can be found in the refrigerated cheese section of most grocery stores.

Wear plastic gloves when working with jalapeño peppers. The juice from the peppers can create a burning sensation on the skin.

Table for Two 101

Almond-Crusted Shrimp

The secret to these delectable shrimp is the almond coating,
which gives them a toasted flavor and satisfying crunch.

PREP TIME: 20 MINUTES   BAKE TIME: 12-13 MINUTES

- 4 **uncooked shell-on jumbo shrimp (about 5 ounces), peeled and deveined**
- 1/2 **cup toasted sliced almonds, chopped**
- 2 **teaspoons all-purpose flour**
- 1 **teaspoon snipped fresh parsley**
- 1/4 **teaspoon salt**
- 1 **tablespoon cornstarch**
- 1 **large egg white**
- 1/4 **cup red plum jam**
- 1/2 **teaspoon Dijon mustard**

1. Preheat oven to 450°F. Peel and devein shrimp, leaving tails on. Using the point of the **Utility Knife**, make a lengthwise cut almost but not all the way through the center of each shrimp. Ease open with fingers. Rinse; pat dry with paper towels.

2. Chop almonds using **Food Chopper**. Place almonds, flour, parsley and salt in shallow dish; mix well. Place cornstarch in separate dish. In **Small Batter Bowl**, beat egg white with **Stainless Mini Whisk** until light and frothy.

3. Holding shrimp by the tail, coat shrimp with cornstarch. Dip shrimp in egg white then in almond mixture to coat. Place shrimp cut-side down, staggering shrimp on **Small Bar Pan**. Lightly spray shrimp with nonstick cooking spray. Bake 12-13 minutes or until shrimp is just cooked through.

4. Meanwhile, combine jam and mustard in **Prep Bowl**. Microwave on HIGH 30-45 seconds or until warm. Serve shrimp immediately with sauce.

Yield: 2 servings

Nutrients per serving: Calories 350, Total Fat 15 g, Saturated Fat 1 g, Cholesterol 40 mg, Carbohydrate 37 g, Protein 19 g, Sodium 670 mg, Fiber 3 g

Diabetic exchanges per serving: 2 1/2 starch, 2 medium-fat meat (2 1/2 carb)

This recipe can be easily doubled and baked on the **Medium Bar Pan**.

To toast almonds in microwave oven, place almonds in the **Small Oval Baker**; microwave on HIGH 1-2 minutes or until golden brown, stirring after 30 seconds. Cool completely.

Use the **Egg Separator**, which conveniently attaches to the rim of most bowls, to separate the egg yolk from the egg white.

To create a beautiful presentation, prop tails of shrimp up with wooden picks before baking. Insert the pick through tail and into the body. Remove before serving.

Florentine Stuffed Chicken Breasts

*A creamy spinach mixture rolled into flattened chicken breasts
makes an elegant main dish for two.*

PREP TIME: 30 MINUTES   COOK TIME: 5-7 MINUTES   BAKE TIME: 25-30 MINUTES

Filling

- ½ **cup chopped fresh mushrooms
  (about 3 medium mushrooms)**
- ⅓ **cup diced red bell pepper**
- 1 **small garlic clove, pressed**
- 1½ **cups packed fresh baby spinach
  leaves, stems removed, coarsely
  chopped**
- ⅛ **teaspoon salt
  Dash of ground black pepper**
- ¼ **cup chive and onion cream cheese
  spread**
- 1½ **teaspoons all-purpose flour**

Chicken and Coating

- 2 **boneless, skinless chicken breast
  halves (6-8 ounces each), flattened
  (see Cook's Tip)**
- 2 **slices firm white sandwich bread,
  grated (½ cup crumbs)**
- 2 **tablespoons (½ ounce) grated fresh
  Parmesan cheese**
- 1 **tablespoon butter or margarine,
  melted**
- 1 **egg white, lightly beaten**

1. Preheat oven to 425°F. For filling, spray
   Small (8-in.) Sauté Pan with nonstick
   cooking spray; heat over medium heat until
   hot. Add mushrooms, bell pepper and garlic
   pressed with **Garlic Press**; cook and stir
   3-4 minutes or until tender. Stir in spinach,
   salt and black pepper; cook and stir 2-3
   minutes or until spinach is completely wilted.

Remove spinach mixture from pan to plate
lined with paper towel; cool slightly. In **Small
Batter Bowl**, combine cream cheese spread,
flour and spinach mixture; mix well and set
aside.

2. For chicken, rinse chicken and pat dry with
   paper towels. Flatten chicken as thinly as
   possible without tearing (see Cook's Tip). For
   coating, using **Deluxe Cheese Grater** fitted
   with coarse grating drum, grate bread. Fit
   grater with fine grating drum and grate
   Parmesan cheese. Combine bread crumbs
   and Parmesan cheese in shallow bowl. Add
   butter and mix until bread crumbs are
   completely coated; set aside.

3. To assemble, divide spinach mixture evenly
   onto center of each chicken breast using
   Large Scoop. Roll up chicken around filling,
   tucking in sides to seal. Generously brush
   chicken bundle with egg white using **Pastry
   Brush**. Place one chicken bundle into coating
   mixture; carefully pat mixture around bundle
   to coat completely. Place seam side down on
   Small Bar Pan. Repeat with remaining
   chicken bundle. Bake 25-30 minutes or until
   coating is deep golden brown and juices run
   clear.

Yield: 2 servings

Nutrients per serving: Calories 490, Total Fat 20 g, Saturated
Fat 11 g, Cholesterol 145 mg, Carbohydrate 24 g, Protein 51 g,
Sodium 790 mg, Fiber 3 g

Diabetic exchanges per serving: 1½ starch, 7 low-fat meat
(1½ carb)

cook's tips

To flatten chicken
breasts, place one
chicken breast half in
resealable plastic food
storage bag and add
1 teaspoon of water (the
water will prevent the
chicken from tearing and
sticking to the bag). Seal
bag; flatten chicken as
thinly as possible without
tearing using flat side of
Meat Tenderizer.
Repeat with remaining
breast half. Discard
plastic bag.

This recipe can be easily
doubled and baked on
the **Medium Bar Pan**.

Mini Italian Meat Loaves

These little meat loaves fit perfectly on the Small Bar Pan. The layer of marinara sauce seals in moisture so the meat loaves stay moist and flavorful.

PREP TIME: 15 MINUTES   BAKE TIME: 26-31 MINUTES

cook's tips

- 2 **tablespoons chopped onion**
- 8 **ounces 90% lean ground beef**
- 2 **tablespoons unseasoned dry bread crumbs**
- 1 **small garlic clove, pressed**
- 1/2 **teaspoon *Pantry Italian Seasoning Mix***
- 1/4 **teaspoon salt**
- 1/8 **teaspoon ground black pepper**
- 1/2 **cup refrigerated marinara sauce, divided**
- 1/4 **cup (1 ounce) shredded Italian cheese blend**

1. Preheat oven to 375°F. Spray **Small Bar Pan** with nonstick cooking spray. Chop onion using **Food Chopper**. In **Stainless (2-qt.) Mixing Bowl**, combine onion, ground beef, bread crumbs, garlic pressed with **Garlic Press**, seasoning mix, salt and black pepper. Add 1/4 cup of the marinara sauce; mix lightly but thoroughly.

2. Shape meat mixture into two small loaves and place on pan; top with remaining marinara sauce. Bake 25-30 minutes or until meat is no longer pink in centers and **Pocket Thermometer** registers 160°F.

3. Sprinkle loaves with cheese; bake 1 minute or just until cheese begins to melt. Remove from oven to serving plates.

Yield: 2 servings

Nutrients per serving: Calories 310, Total Fat 17 g, Saturated Fat 7 g, Cholesterol 85 mg, Carbohydrate 11 g, Protein 28 g, Sodium 750 mg, Fiber 1 g

Diabetic exchanges per serving: 1/2 starch, 4 low-fat meat, 1 fat (1/2 carb)

Variation: *Family-Size Italian Meat Loaf:* The ingredients in this recipe can be increased to make 6 servings. Spray **Stoneware Loaf Pan** with nonstick cooking spray. Combine 1 1/2 pounds ground beef, 1/2 cup chopped onions, 1/3 cup bread crumbs, 1 egg, 2 pressed garlic cloves, 1 1/2 teaspoons seasoning mix, 3/4 teaspoon salt and 1/4 teaspoon ground black pepper. Stir in half of a 15-ounce container refrigerated marinara sauce; mix lightly but thoroughly. Shape meat mixture into loaf in pan. Top with remaining sauce. Bake 55-60 minutes or until meat is no longer pink in center of loaf and internal temperature reaches 160°F. Sprinkle with 1/2 cup cheese; bake 3 minutes or just until cheese begins to melt. Remove meat loaf to serving platter.

Italian seasoning can be substituted for the Italian Seasoning Mix, if desired.

Italian cheese blend is a mixture of up to six different cheeses. These include mozzarella, provolone, Parmesan, Romano, fontina and/or Asiago. Italian cheese blend is a quick way to add flavor to pizzas, sandwiches and pasta dishes.

Chiles Rellenos Chicken

This popular Mexican menu item, translated as "stuffed peppers," is rearranged and served over chicken breasts with a fun nacho cheese chip crust.

PREP TIME: 15 MINUTES   BAKE TIME: 22-25 MINUTES

2 **boneless, skinless chicken breast halves (4-6 ounces each)**

1 **lime, cut in half crosswise**

1 **egg white**

1 **garlic clove, pressed**

1/2 **cup finely crushed nacho cheese flavored tortilla chips (about 1 1/2 cups chips)**

1/2 **can (4 ounces) whole green chiles, drained and cut into strips**

2 **tablespoons shredded Monterey Jack cheese**

1 **teaspoon snipped fresh cilantro**
  Prepared salsa (optional)

1. Preheat oven to 400°F. Spray **Small Bar Pan** with nonstick cooking spray. Rinse chicken and pat dry with paper towels. Place one chicken breast half in resealable plastic food storage bag; seal bag. Lightly flatten chicken to even thickness using flat side of **Meat Tenderizer**. Repeat with remaining chicken breast half. Discard plastic bag.

2. Juice lime halves into **Small Batter Bowl** using **Citrus Press**. Add egg white and garlic pressed with **Garlic Press**; whisk until frothy using **Stainless Whisk**.

3. Place tortilla chips in another resealable plastic food storage bag and finely crush using flat side of Meat Tenderizer. Place crushed chips in shallow dish. Dip chicken breasts into egg mixture and then into chips, coating completely. Discard any remaining crushed chips. Place chicken on pan.

4. Bake 20-22 minutes or until chicken is no longer pink and juices run clear. Arrange chile strips over chicken; sprinkle with cheese. Bake 2-3 minutes or just until cheese melts. Remove from oven. Sprinkle with cilantro. Serve with salsa, if desired.

Yield: 2 servings

Nutrients per serving: Calories 530, Total Fat 22 g, Saturated Fat 5 g, Cholesterol 75 mg, Carbohydrate 48 g, Protein 36 g, Sodium 700 mg, Fiber 4 g

Diabetic exchanges per serving: 3 starch, 4 medium-fat meat (3 carb)

cook's tips

The ingredients in this recipe can be easily doubled and baked on the **Medium Bar Pan**.

The Citrus Press makes juicing limes a quick and easy task. Simply slice a lime in half crosswise, place it into the hopper of the press and squeeze.

Traditional chiles rellenos start with mild poblano peppers that are stuffed with Chihuahua cheese, then dipped in an egg batter or breaded and fried.

South Pacific Salad

*This Pan-Asian, gourmet salad is worthy of special occasions
such as birthdays and promotions.*

PREP TIME: 15 MINUTES   BAKE TIME: 10-12 MINUTES   COOL TIME: 10 MINUTES

cook's tips

Wontons

- 1/4 **cup coarsely chopped macadamia nuts, divided**
- 4 **(7 x 7-inch) egg roll wrappers, divided**
- 4 **teaspoons corn syrup, divided**
- 1 **teaspoon black sesame seeds, divided**

Salad

- 1 **medium carrot, peeled and cut into julienne strips**
- 1/2 **small red bell pepper, sliced into thin strips**
- 1 **can (11 ounces) mandarin oranges, drained**
- 1 **cup sugar snap peas**
- 2 **cups chopped cooked chicken**
- 2 **cups (3 ounces) European mix salad blend of lettuce and baby greens**
- 2 **tablespoons low-fat sesame-ginger salad dressing**

1. Preheat oven to 375°F. For wontons, coarsely chop macadamia nuts with **Food Chopper**. Place two egg roll wrappers on **Rectangle Stone**. Drizzle 1 teaspoon corn syrup over each wrapper; spread syrup evenly over entire surface with **Small Spreader**. Sprinkle each wrapper with 1 tablespoon nuts and 1/4 teaspoon sesame seeds. Bake 10-12 minutes or until golden brown. Using **Large Serving Spatula**, remove wontons to **Stackable Cooling Rack**. Cool completely. Repeat with remaining wrappers.

2. For salad, using **Julienne Peeler**, cut carrot into julienne strips then cut into matchstick pieces. Slice bell pepper into thin strips using **Chef's Knife**. Place carrot, bell pepper, oranges, peas, chicken and greens in large **Colander Bowl**. Drizzle with salad dressing; toss to coat.

3. Place two wontons on two **Simple Additions**™ **Medium Squares**; top each wonton with half of the salad mixture. Top with remaining wontons. Serve immediately with additional dressing, if desired.

Yield: 2 servings

Nutrients per serving: Calories 650, Total Fat 24 g, Saturated Fat 4.5 g, Cholesterol 105 mg, Carbohydrate 66 g, Protein 46 g, Sodium 650 mg, Fiber 8 g

Diabetic exchanges per serving: 4 starch, 1 vegetable, 5 low-fat meat (4 carb)

This recipe can easily be doubled and baked on the **Rectangle Stone**.

Sesame seeds are available in several colors such as black, tan, red and the widely available ivory. Toasted sesame seeds can be substituted for the black sesame seeds, if desired.

To prepare your own *Asian Dressing*, combine 1/3 cup rice vinegar, 3 tablespoons soy sauce, 2 teaspoons sugar, 1 pressed garlic clove, 1/4 teaspoon ground ginger and 3/4 cup vegetable oil in **Measure, Mix, & Pour**™ or **Small Batter Bowl**; whisk until blended. Refrigerate until ready to use.

Bacon, Tomato & Swiss Quiche

Create-a-Quiche

Quiche doesn't have to be a part of a big brunch gathering. Here, you have options to make one of three amazing crustless quiches for yourself and one special guest.

PREP TIME: 15 MINUTES   BAKE TIME: 30-35 MINUTES

Quiche Base	3 eggs ½ cup half and half 2 tablespoons all-purpose flour		¼ teaspoon salt Dash of ground black pepper
	Bacon, Tomato & Swiss	**Spinach, Mushroom & Provolone**	**Ham, Broccoli & Cheddar**
Filling Ingredients	3 bacon slices, crisply cooked, drained and crumbled ⅓ cup seeded, chopped plum tomato 2 tablespoons thinly sliced green onion	½ package (10 ounces) frozen chopped spinach, thawed, well drained and patted dry (½ cup) ⅓ cup chopped fresh mushrooms ¼ cup chopped red bell pepper	½ cup chopped cooked smoked ham ⅓ cup chopped fresh broccoli 2 tablespoons finely chopped onion
Cheese	½ cup (2 ounces) shredded Swiss cheese	½ cup (2 ounces) shredded Provolone cheese	½ cup (2 ounces) shredded sharp cheddar cheese

1. Preheat oven to 375°F. Spray **Small Oval Baker** with nonstick cooking spray. Whisk together **Quiche Base** ingredients in **Classic Batter Bowl**; set aside.

2. Combine **Filling Ingredients** and **Cheese**; spoon into bottom of baker. Pour **Quiche Base** over **Filling Ingredients**.

3. Bake 30-35 minutes or until center is set. (A knife inserted in center will come out clean.) Let stand 5 minutes before serving. Cut in half and serve.

Yield: 2 servings

Nutrients per serving:

Bacon, Tomato & Swiss	Spinach, Mushroom & Provolone	Ham, Broccoli & Cheddar
Calories 370, Total Fat 26 g, Saturated Fat 13 g, Cholesterol 375 mg, Carbohydrate 11 g, Protein 23 g, Sodium 680 mg, Fiber less than 1 g	Calories 360, Total Fat 22 g, Saturated Fat 11 g, Cholesterol 360 mg, Carbohydrate 15 g, Protein 24 g, Sodium 1010 mg, Fiber 3 g	Calories 370, Total Fat 24 g, Saturated Fat 13 g, Cholesterol 390 mg, Carbohydrate 12 g, Protein 25 g, Sodium 870 mg, Fiber less than 1 g
Diabetic exchanges per serving: 0 starch, 2 vegetable, 3 medium-fat meat, 2 fat (0 carb)	Diabetic exchanges per serving: 0 starch, 3 vegetable, 3 medium-fat meat, 1 fat (0 carb)	Diabetic exchanges per serving: 0 starch, 2 vegetable, 3 medium-fat meat, 2 fat (0 carb)

cook's tips

Provolone cheese is a southern Italian cheese that has a firm texture and a mild, smoky flavor. It can be found in the deli section of the supermarket. Italian cheese blend or mozzarella cheese can be substituted for the Provolone cheese, if desired.

To cook bacon in the microwave, line a paper plate with a paper towel. Place bacon slices on paper towel; cover with another paper towel. Place paper plate in microwave; microwave on HIGH 45-60 seconds or until bacon is cooked through and crisp.

This recipe can be easily doubled and baked in the **Deep Dish Pie Plate**. Bake at 375°F 45-50 minutes or until center is set.

Table for Two 113

German Apple Pancake

Why spend money at a restaurant for breakfast when you can create a delicious baked apple pancake at home?

PREP TIME: 30 MINUTES   BAKE TIME: 20-23 MINUTES

Apple Filling

- **1 small Granny Smith apple**
- **2 teaspoons butter or margarine**
- **¼ cup packed brown sugar**
- **1 teaspoon *Pantry Korintje Cinnamon***

Pancake

- **½ cup all-purpose flour**
- **1 tablespoon granulated sugar**
- **¼ teaspoon salt**
- **2 eggs**
- **½ cup milk**
- **2 teaspoons butter or margarine, melted**
- **Powdered sugar or warm maple syrup (optional)**

1. Preheat oven to 400°F. Spray **Small Oval Baker** with nonstick cooking spray. For apple filling, peel, core and slice apple using **Apple Peeler/Corer/Slicer**. Cut apple slices into quarters. Melt butter in **Small (8-in.) Sauté Pan** over medium heat. Add apple, brown sugar and cinnamon. Cook 20 minutes or until apple is very tender and most of the liquid has evaporated.

2. Meanwhile, for pancake, combine flour, granulated sugar and salt in **Classic Batter Bowl**. In **Small Batter Bowl**, whisk together eggs, milk and melted butter using **Stainless Whisk**. Add egg mixture to flour mixture; whisk until dry ingredients are moistened. (Batter will be slightly lumpy.) Pour batter into baker. Spoon apple mixture evenly over batter. Bake 20-23 minutes or until puffed and golden brown. Remove from oven; sprinkle with powdered sugar, if desired. Cut into wedges and serve with maple syrup, if desired.

Yield: 2 servings

Nutrients per serving: Calories 430, Total Fat 14 g, Saturated Fat 7 g, Cholesterol 235 mg, Carbohydrate 69 g, Protein 12 g, Sodium 460 mg, Fiber 3 g

Diabetic exchanges per serving: 4 starch, ½ fruit, 2 fat (4½ carb)

cook's tips

Ground cinnamon can be substituted for the Korintje Cinnamon, if desired.

The German pancake, also known as a Dutch baby, is a baked pancake that rises dramatically in the oven.

Western Brunch Pizza

*The sloped sides of the Small Round Stone make this
egg dish easy to prepare and serve.*

PREP TIME: 15 MINUTES   BAKE TIME: 12-15 MINUTES

1   **package (4 ounces) refrigerated
crescent rolls**

1   **egg, lightly beaten**

2   **ounces diced deli ham (1/4 cup)**

1/4   **cup diced green bell pepper or
poblano pepper**

1   **tablespoon thinly sliced green onion
with top**

1/2   **cup (2 ounces) shredded Colby
& Monterey Jack cheese blend**

2   **tablespoons diced plum tomato**

**Salt and ground black pepper
(optional)**

1. Preheat oven to 375°F. Unroll crescent
dough; separate into two rectangles. Arrange
rectangles edge to edge on lightly floured
Small Round Stone to form a square. Using
lightly floured **Baker's Roller™**, roll dough to
within 1 inch of edge of stone. Fold in
1/2 inch of edge of dough to create rim.

2. In **Small Batter Bowl**, whisk egg using
Stainless Mini Whisk. Sprinkle ham, bell
pepper and green onion evenly over dough;
drizzle egg evenly over pizza. Sprinkle with
cheese. Bake 12-15 minutes or until crust is
golden brown and filling is set in center.

3. Remove from oven. Sprinkle with tomato;
season with salt and black pepper, if desired.
Slice into wedges using **Pizza Cutter**.
Serve warm.

Yield: 2 servings

Nutrients per serving: Calories 390, Total Fat 23 g, Saturated
Fat 10g, Cholesterol 145 mg, Carbohydrate 26 g, Protein 19 g,
Sodium 1040 mg, Fiber less than 1 g

Diabetic exchanges per serving: 1½ starch, 1 vegetable,
1½ medium-fat meat, 3 fat (1½ carb)

cook's tips

minutes or less

The Small Round Stone
and our other flat
Stoneware is perfect
for making pizza.
Stoneware's even
heating and heat
retention properties will
garner a crisp crust
every time.

Poblano peppers are
dark green chiles with a
rich flavor that ranges
from mild to slightly
spicy. In general, the
darker the pepper, the
stronger the flavor.
Poblanos are about
2½ inches wide and
4-5 inches long, forming
a triangular shape.

Cooked, sliced sausage,
cooked, crumbled bacon
or diced cooked potatoes
can be substituted for
the ham, if desired.

Chocolate-Peanut Butter Torte

*Mayonnaise and applesauce provide moisture and
tenderness in this dramatic cake.*

PREP TIME: 20 MINUTES   BAKE TIME: 22-25 MINUTES   COOL TIME: 1 HOUR

cook's tips

Cake

- 1 **package (9 ounces) devil's food cake mix**
- 2 **tablespoons unsweetened cocoa powder**
- 2 **tablespoons mayonnaise**
- 1 **egg**
- 1/2 **cup unsweetened applesauce**

Glaze

- 1/3 **cup semi-sweet chocolate morsels**
- 2 **tablespoons heavy whipping cream**
- 2 **tablespoons caramel ice cream topping**
- 2 **tablespoons creamy peanut butter, divided**
- **Spanish peanuts (optional)**

1. Preheat oven to 350°F. For cake, lightly spray **Small Bar Pan** with nonstick cooking spray. Cut a piece of **Parchment Paper** to cover bottom of pan. Line pan with Parchment Paper; lightly spray with cooking spray. In **Classic Batter Bowl**, whisk cake mix and cocoa powder using **Stainless Whisk**. Add mayonnaise, egg and applesauce; whisk until well blended. Pour batter into pan. Bake 22-25 minutes or until **Cake Tester** inserted in center comes out clean. Remove from oven to **Stackable Cooling Rack**; cool 5 minutes. Remove from pan; cover with clean **Kitchen Towel** and cool completely.

2. For glaze, combine chocolate morsels, whipping cream, ice cream topping and 1 tablespoon of the peanut butter in **Small Micro-Cooker®**. Microwave on HIGH 15-30 seconds or until melted; stir until smooth. Set aside. Place remaining peanut butter in **Prep Bowl**. Microwave on HIGH 10-20 seconds or until melted and smooth; set aside.

3. To assemble torte, using **Serrated Bread Knife**, cut cake in half crosswise to form two equal layers. Carefully place one layer on top of the other and trim to match edges. Place one layer onto serving plate. Spread half of the glaze over bottom layer using **Small Spreader**, allowing glaze to drip down sides. Top with second cake layer. Repeat with remaining glaze. Drizzle with melted peanut butter and swirl into glaze using **Quikut Paring Knife**. If desired, sprinkle peanuts around bottom of torte. Slice using **Utility Knife** dipped in hot water.

Yield: 4 servings

Nutrients per serving: Calories 560, Total Fat 27 g,
Saturated Fat 10 g, Cholesterol 105 mg, Carbohydrate 71 g,
Protein 10 g, Sodium 660 mg, Fiber 4 g

Diabetic exchanges per serving: 3 starch, 1 1/2 fruit, 5 fat
(4 1/2 carb)

If desired, half of a standard devil's food cake mix (9 ounces or 1 3/4 cups dry mix) can be substituted for the 9-ounce package of cake mix.

This recipe can be easily doubled and baked in the **Medium Bar Pan** using an 18.25-ounce package of devil's food cake mix. Bake at 350°F 28-32 minutes; proceed as recipe directs.

To easily drizzle peanut butter over top of torte, pour melted peanut butter into corner of small resealable plastic food storage bag. Twist top of bag secure. Cut a small tip off corner of bag to allow the peanut butter to flow through.

Pear and Cranberry Crisp

This home-style, streusel-topped dessert is perfect for a cool, autumn day.

cook's tips

PREP TIME: 15 MINUTES   BAKE TIME: 30-32 MINUTES   STAND TIME: 15 MINUTES

Filling

- 2 **tablespoons thawed, frozen cranberry juice concentrate**
- 1/2 **cup sweetened dried cranberries**
- 2 **medium pears**
- 1 **tablespoon sugar**

Streusel Topping

- 2 **tablespoons butter or margarine, melted**
- 2 **tablespoons chopped almonds**
- 1/3 **cup all-purpose flour**
- 2 **tablespoons sugar**
- 1/4 **teaspoon ground cinnamon**
  Thawed, frozen whipped topping or vanilla ice cream (optional)

1. Preheat oven to 375°F. For filling, microwave juice concentrate in **Small Micro-Cooker®** on HIGH 15-25 seconds or until boiling. Stir in cranberries; let stand 10 minutes to soften.

2. Meanwhile, core and slice pears with **Apple Wedger**; cut slices in half crosswise using **Paring Knife**. Combine cranberry mixture, pears and sugar; toss gently. Spoon filling into **Small Oval Baker**.

3. For streusel topping, microwave butter in **Small Batter Bowl** on HIGH 15-25 seconds or until melted. Chop almonds using **Food Chopper**. Add almonds, flour, sugar and cinnamon; mix well. Sprinkle streusel evenly over filling.

4. Bake 30-32 minutes or until streusel is golden brown. Remove from oven; cool 15 minutes. Serve with whipped topping or vanilla ice cream, if desired.

Yield: 2 servings

Nutrients per serving: Calories 530, Total Fat 17 g, Saturated Fat 8 g, Cholesterol 30 mg, Carbohydrate 96 g, Protein 5 g, Sodium 85 mg, Fiber 7 g

Diabetic exchanges per serving: 2 starch, 4 fruit, 3 fat (6 carb)

This recipe can easily be doubled and baked in the **Mini-Baker**. Bake at 375°F 45-47 minutes or until streusel is golden brown.

Frozen juice concentrates usually come in 12-ounce cans. When using 2 tablespoons concentrate for this recipe, the remaining juice concentrate can be mixed with 4 cups cold water in our **Family-Size Quick-Stir®️ Pitcher**.

Common varieties of pears, such as Anjou, Bartlett and Bosc, are delicious when eaten either raw or cooked. Choose pears that are fragrant and free of blemishes.

Berry-Vanilla Shortcakes

*Sweet and simple, these home-style shortcakes
are filled with summer's best berries.*

PREP TIME: 15 MINUTES   BAKE TIME: 17-19 MINUTES   COOL TIME: 20 MINUTES

Shortcakes

- 2/3 **cup all-purpose flour**
- 1 **teaspoon sugar**
- 1/2 **teaspoon baking powder**
- 1/4 **teaspoon salt**
- 1/2 **cup heavy whipping cream**

Filling

- 1 **cup assorted fresh berries, such as sliced strawberries, blackberries or raspberries**
- 2 **tablespoons sugar**
- 1/4 **teaspoon *Pantry Double Strength Vanilla***
- **Sweetened whipped cream (optional, see Cook's Tip)**
- **Fresh mint (optional)**

1. Preheat oven to 450°F. For shortcakes, combine flour, sugar, baking powder and salt in **Classic Batter Bowl**. Add whipping cream; stir just until a soft dough forms. Spoon onto **Small Bar Pan**, forming two equal mounds; pat down lightly. If desired, brush tops with a small amount of additional cream and lightly sprinkle with additional sugar. Bake 17-19 minutes or until golden brown; remove from oven. Remove shortcakes from pan to **Stackable Cooling Rack**; cool completely.

2. Meanwhile, for filling, gently toss berries with sugar and vanilla in **Small Batter Bowl**; let stand at least 30 minutes.

3. Split shortcakes in half horizontally using **Serrated Bread Knife**. For each serving, place bottom half of shortcake onto serving plate; top with half of the berry mixture. Top with a dollop of sweetened whipped cream, if desired. Cover with top half of shortcake. Garnish with mint, if desired.

Yield: 2 servings

Nutrients per serving: Calories 430, Total Fat 21 g, Saturated Fat 12 g, Cholesterol 80 mg, Carbohydrate 59 g, Protein 5 g, Sodium 430 mg, Fiber 4 g

Diabetic exchanges per serving: 2 starch, 1½ fruit, 4 fat (3½ carb)

cook's tips

The sugar that is sprinkled over the shortcakes can burn onto the surface of the stone. Line the bar pan with a piece of **Parchment Paper** for easy clean-up.

To make sweetened whipped cream, combine ¼ cup heavy whipping cream, 1 tablespoon of sugar and ⅛ teaspoon Pantry Double Strength Vanilla in a chilled **Stainless (2-qt.) Mixing Bowl**. Beat on high speed of electric mixer until soft peaks form. (Tips of peaks will curl down when beaters are lifted.)

If desired, ½ teaspoon vanilla can be substituted for the Double Strength Vanilla in the berry mixture, and ¼ teaspoon vanilla can be substituted for the Double Strength Vanilla in the sweetened whipped cream.

Raspberry-Lime Meringues

*Delicate meringue shells hold cool sorbet and kiwi slices, creating
a dramatic finish to any special meal.*

PREP TIME: 20 MINUTES   BAKE TIME: 1 HOUR, 30 MINUTES   COOL TIME: 2 HOURS OR OVERNIGHT

cook's tips

Meringue Shells

- 2 **large egg whites, room temperature**
- 1/8 **teaspoon cream of tartar**
- 1/3 **cup granulated sugar**

Sauce and Filling

- 1 **lime**
- 3 **scoops (3/4 cup) raspberry sorbet, divided**
- 1 **kiwi, peeled, sliced and quartered**

1. Preheat oven to 200°F. Cut a piece of **Parchment Paper** to cover bottom of **Small Bar Pan**. Draw two 3-inch squares with pencil on Parchment Paper, spacing evenly. Turn paper over and line bottom of pan.

2. For meringue shells, in **Classic Batter Bowl**, beat egg whites on high speed of electric mixer until very foamy, about 20 seconds. Add cream of tartar and continue to beat until soft peaks form, about 1 minute. (Tips of peaks will curl down when beaters are lifted.) While continuously beating on high speed, gradually add sugar in a slow, steady stream. (Do not add all of the sugar at once.) Continue beating on high speed until sugar is dissolved, mixture is glossy and stiff peaks form, 3-4 minutes. (Tips of peaks will remain upright when beaters are lifted.)

3. Attach open star tip to **Easy Accent®Decorator**; fill with meringue mixture. Pipe meringue mixture onto squares on Parchment Paper, filling in squares to form bases for shells. (Bases should be about 1/2 inch thick.) Pipe 2-3 rows of meringue mixture onto edges of squares, building up sides to form shells. Bake 1 hour, 30 minutes or until dry. (Meringue shells will not brown.) Turn oven off. Cool shells in oven with oven door closed at least 2 hours or overnight.

4. For sauce, finely grate lime using **Microplane® Adjustable Grater** to measure 1/2 teaspoon zest. Place 1 scoop (1/4 cup) of the sorbet in **Prep Bowl**; microwave on HIGH 20-30 seconds or until melted. Stir in lime zest. Place meringue shells on serving plates. Fill each shell with half of the sauce and 1 scoop of the remaining sorbet using **Ice Cream Dipper**. Top sorbet with sliced kiwi and serve immediately.

Yield: 2 servings

| LIGHT | Nutrients per serving: Calories 260, Total Fat 0 g, Saturated Fat 0 g, Cholesterol 0 mg, Carbohydrate 62 g, Protein 4 g, Sodium 55 mg, Fiber 3 g |

Diabetic exchanges per serving: 1 starch, 3 fruit (4 carb)

For best results, choose a cool, dry day for making meringue shells.

While eggs are still cold, separate with the **Egg Separator** that conveniently attaches to the Classic Batter Bowl. Eggs separate best when at refrigerated temperature, but egg whites beat to their fullest volume at room temperature. Don't let even a speck of yolk get into whites, or they will not beat properly.

For a beautiful garnish, dip a slice of lime into sugar to coat edges and twist.

Recipe Index

Stoneware Index

About Our Recipes

All recipes were developed and tested in The Pampered Chef® Test Kitchens by professional home economists. For best results, we recommend you use the ingredients indicated in the recipe. The preparation and cooking times at the beginning of each recipe serve as a helpful guide when planning your time in the kitchen. Some of our recipes can be prepared in 30 minutes or less and are accompanied by a symbol indicating this. As an important first step, we suggest you read through the recipe and assemble the necessary ingredients and equipment. "Prep time" is the approximate amount of time needed to prepare recipe ingredients before a final "Cook" or "Bake time." Prep time includes active steps such as chopping and mixing. It can also include cooking ingredients for a recipe that is assembled and then baked. Some preparation steps can be done simultaneously or during cooking and are usually indicated by the term "meanwhile." Some recipes that have steps not easily separated have a combined "Prep and cook time."

Notes on Nutrition

The nutrition information in *Stoneware Inspirations* can help you decide how specific recipes can fit into your overall meal plan. The nutrient values for each recipe were derived from The Food Processor, Version 8.3.0 (ESHA Research), or are provided by food manufacturers. In addition to listing calories, total fat, saturated fat, cholesterol, carbohydrate, protein, sodium and fiber, we include diabetic exchanges commonly used by people with diabetes. **This information is based on the most current dietary guidelines, *Exchange Lists for Meal Planning (2003)*, by the American Diabetes Association and the American Dietetic Association.** For each recipe, two lists of exchanges are provided. The first option is based on the traditional method of figuring diabetic exchanges; the second option is given in parentheses and reflects the newer system of carbohydrate counting. When using either approach to meal planning, always consult with your physician, registered dietician, or certified diabetes educator, who will address your individual needs.

Nutritional analysis for each recipe is based on the first ingredient listed whenever a choice is given and does not include optional ingredients, garnishes, fat used to grease pans, or serving suggestions. The ingredients used in our recipes and for nutritional analyses are based on most commonly purchased foods and, unless indicated otherwise, use 2 percent reduced-fat milk and large eggs. Recipes requiring ground beef are analyzed based on 90 or 95 percent lean ground beef. When margarine is an ingredient option, use a product containing 80 percent fat and not vegetable spread. Recipes labeled as [LIGHT] contain 30 percent or fewer calories from fat.

Metric Conversion Chart

Volume Measurements (dry)	Volume Measurements (fluid)	Dimensions
⅛ teaspoon = 0.6 mL	1 fluid ounce (2 tablespoons) = 30 mL	⅛ inch = 3 mm
¼ teaspoon = 1.25 mL	4 fluid ounces (½ cup) = 125 mL	¼ inch = 6 mm
½ teaspoon = 2.5 mL	8 fluid ounces (1 cup) = 250 mL	½ inch = 1 cm
¾ teaspoon = 3.75 mL	12 fluid ounces (1½ cups) = 375 mL	¾ inch = 2 cm
1 teaspoon = 5 mL	16 fluid ounces (2 cups) = 500 mL	1 inch = 2.5 cm
1 tablespoon = 15 mL		**Oven Temperatures**
2 tablespoons = 30 mL	**Weights (mass)**	250°F = 120°C
¼ cup = 50 mL	1 ounce = 30 g	275°F = 140°C
⅓ cup = 75 mL	4 ounces = 125 g	300°F = 150°C
½ cup = 125 mL	8 ounces = 250 g	325°F = 160°C
⅔ cup = 150 mL	12 ounces = 350 g	350°F = 180°C
¾ cup = 175 mL	16 ounces = 1 pound = 500 g	375°F = 190°C
1 cup = 250 mL		400°F = 200°C
		425°F = 220°C
		450°F = 230°C

Recipes in this cookbook have not been tested using metric measures. When converting and preparing recipes with metric measures, some variations in quality may be noticed.